THE DAILY WAD

CHOICE TIDBITS TO ENJOY
THROUGHOUT YOUR DAY

PAUL ANDERSON

WestBow
PRESS
A DIVISION OF THOMAS NELSON

WestBow Press books may be ordered through booksellers or by contacting:
WestBow Press
A Division of Thomas Nelson
1663 Liberty Drive
Bloomington, IN 47403
www.westbowpress.com
1-(866) 928-1240

ISBN: 978-1-4497-4370-3 (hc)
ISBN: 978-1-4497-4371-0 (sc)
ISBN: 978-1-4497-4372-7 (e)

Library of Congress Control Number: 2012905138
Printed in the United States of America

WestBow Press rev. date: 04/17/2012

My purpose in writing this book is to encourage and assure you that the grace of God is with you no matter what happens.

(1 Peter 5:12b NLT)

PREFACE

Some years ago, I noticed that certain verses—and even brief phrases—seemed to stand out from the Bible passages I read during my daily devotions. I found myself thinking about, meditating on, and ruminating over the words throughout the day. It amused me to picture myself "chewing my cud." I shouldn't have been surprised. The Bible does say, "We are his people, the sheep of his pasture" (Psalm 100:3b NIV), and sheep chew a cud.

Other pictures came to my mind—a baseball player chewing a wad of bubblegum; an old codger chewing a chaw of tobacco. The more delicate expression would be in reference to Mary, the mother of Jesus. Of her the Scriptures record, "But Mary treasured up all these things and *pondered* them in her heart" (Luke 2:19 NIV). The meaning is the same: "You thrill to God's Word, you chew on Scripture day and night" (Psalm 1:2-3, The Message).

So was born my daily wad. I wrote the phrases on cards, thought about the words throughout the day, and shared them with others when the opportunity presented itself. I was blessed, and others were blessed. My prayer is that you will be blessed as you read, ruminate, and are refreshed by *The Daily Wad*.

Paul I. Anderson, 2012

January 1

The land you are . . . to take possession of is a land of mountains and valleys that drinks rain from heaven. It is a land the LORD your God cares for; the eyes of the LORD your God are continually on it from the beginning of the year to its end (Deuteronomy 11:11-12).

I believe Moses' description of the Promised Land is parallel to what I might see if permitted to gaze into the future. The coming year is a "land" to be taken and possessed for the glory of God. "Promised" does not mean it will come easy. It is "a land of mountains and valleys"—highs and lows—and no two days are exactly alike. But there will be an outpouring and refreshing of the Spirit from heaven. It will be under God's care from the first day to the last.

I can move into the new year, seeing it as a land filled with God's promise, provision, and presence. I am expecting to take possession of it in His name and for His glory. It will be a good year!

January 2

"You, my sheep, the sheep of my pasture, are people, and I am your God," declares the Sovereign LORD (Ezekiel 34:31).

The Lord says things differently than we do. A minister might say something like, "You, my congregation, are sheep to be pastured, shorn, or sent to market." We tend to go from the actual to the figurative, ending with the characteristics that please or irritate us. But God goes from the figurative to the actual. Yes, we are like sheep. We are under the care of a shepherd, we are protected from predators by His presence, we belong to a flock, and we have intrinsic value. God says in actuality we are *people*, not animals—His people whom He loves, cares for, and values.

January 3

I will be glad and rejoice in your love, for you saw my affliction and knew the anguish of my soul (Psalm 31:7).

The Lord sees my affliction and knows my anguish. The word *knew* speaks of more than intellectual facts. It is a word having ties to the most loving and intimate of physical relationships between a husband and his wife. It speaks of closeness, an "entering into." David saw this as proof of God's love and concern for him. Loving us as He does, He notices everything that has become a painful burden. Some of this suffering may be physical, but there is pain that goes beyond that. The writer to the Hebrews reminds us: "For we have not a high priest which cannot be touched with the feeling of our infirmities" (Hebrews 4:15 KJV). The Scriptures say Jesus was often "moved with compassion." He sees, knows, and cares!

January 4

Brothers, if you have a message of encouragement for the people, please speak (Acts 13:15).

Not every message is pleasant to hear, but later on, like discipline, if received and acted upon, it "produces a harvest of righteousness and peace" (Hebrews 12:11).

Good parents realize there is more to be said to their children than directives and correctives. Children require a lot of encouragement. Speaking for myself, I generally know when and where I've done wrong. I may need a reminder from time to time, but nagging gets old real fast. Sometimes I've gone to church with emotional bumps, bruises, and gaping wounds and didn't feel like listening to another lecture on what I did wrong. I'm thankful for every message of encouragement I've heard over my lifetime. Lord, bless those brothers and sisters!

JANUARY 5

He wrote down the substance of his dream (Daniel 7:1).

I must take care when I repeat what I believe the Lord has spoken or shown to me, as it is as easy to embellish as it is to forget—perhaps easier. Daniel was given many visions and dreams, heavy with meaning. Some came during the night hours. So he would not forget important details, "he wrote down the substance of his dream," recording the essence of what he had seen and heard.

The practice of journaling does this for me. I need to write down the essence of those experiences when I sense the Lord is giving me insight or preparing me for something He wants to do. I don't journal on a daily basis—not every day merits that—but if I think I can rely solely on my memory to get it right and keep it right, I'm only fooling myself. As I journal more often, I stay fresh.

JANUARY 6

Those who cling to worthless idols forfeit the grace that could be theirs (Jonah 2:8).

The most innocuous thing that can be said about idols is that they are worthless, and the most offensive thing that can be said about idols is that they deprive us of "the grace that could be ours."

Idolaters are fools; they break the first two of the Ten Commandments. I do not need to bow before or sacrifice to a sculptured image of a heathen god to be an idolater. All I need do is substitute the one true God with something—anything—else. My choice would be futile, pointless, and useless. Worst of all, I would dishonor God and lose the very help I know I need. "So let us come boldly to the throne of our gracious God. There we will receive his mercy, and we will find grace to help us when we need it" (Hebrews 4:16 NLT). I must let go of all else and cling only to the Lord. His grace is sufficient!

JANUARY 7

He makes me lie down in green pastures (Psalm 23:2).

I remember when my mother told me it was time for a nap. I also remember not agreeing with her. I was having too much fun. I was too busy. I didn't have time for a nap. I protested her announcement. I whined, I cried, I threw a tantrum. But she was insistent. There was no giving in on her part. She made me lie down for a nap. The best I could get out of her would be, "You just lie there with your eyes closed for at least fifteen minutes. You can get up after you have slept." Aha! I could still win this deal.

Finally, I complied. I closed my eyes—much too tightly—and lay on my bed. I could do this. The next thing I knew, I was awake and an hour or two had slipped away. I felt happier and refreshed.

Sometimes the Good Shepherd has to make me lie down. It is for my good. I will thank Him for it later.

JANUARY 8

For the Scripture says to Pharaoh: "I raised you up for this very purpose, that I might display my power in you and that my name might be proclaimed in all the earth" (Romans 9:17).

Amazing! God has a purpose for every person. I would agree that is true of you, and I can accept that is true of me. But ungodly world leaders? I would think I should do all I can to make sure they never gain that place of power. And if they do, my prayer should be that they be removed as soon as possible.

Do I ever think that maybe it is the will of God for men and women who are far from Him to occupy positions of authority and influence? It doesn't mean I am to agree with everything, or even anything, they do. My responsibility is to live for the glory of God and pray that God's purpose for others will be fulfilled as well.

January 9

Do not gloat over me, my enemy! Though I have fallen, I will rise (Micah 7:8).

I've seen his smirk. I've heard his sneer. I've tried to block out his mocking laughter. He seemed so sympathetic when I was struggling with the temptation. He offered the easy way out. He suggested the quickest, feel-good solution. And when I fell, he roared his sarcasm and bellowed his condemnation. But I will not let the Enemy have the last word! I will not offer excuses in place of confession and repentance.

David said "Against you, you only, have I sinned and done what is evil in your sight" (Psalm 51:4). The Enemy would like the fallen to think all is lost. Not so. "Though I have fallen, I will rise . . ." "He lifted me out of the pit of despair, out of the mud and the mire. He set my feet on solid ground and steadied me as I walked along" (Psalm 40:2 NLT). I will get up!

January 10

The LORD . . . delights in the well-being of his servant (Psalm 35:27).

Well-being speaks of one's health. Jesus spoke of one's well-being as being made "whole" (John 5:6 KJV). If something is whole, it is in one piece; it is not fragmented, nor are any parts omitted or missing.

Wholeness involves more than my physical health. My "being" includes my spirit, soul, and body, so well-being addresses my spiritual, mental, physical, and social health. When I am healthy, there is balance as well as completeness. Not only are all the parts present, they are in proper proportion and function with all the other parts. This is what the Lord wants for me today. He delights in the well-being and wholeness that makes me a faithful, contributing servant. Do I equally desire to be made whole—to be well in every area of my life? That is the well-being the Lord delights in.

JANUARY 11

> Think of what you were when you were called (1 Corinthians 1:16).

The glorious reality is that I have been called—called by God. There is no higher honor. To think the God of the universe would call me, would choose me, would desire to use me for His glory is beyond my wildest dreams. (That ought to look good on my résumé! Do I dare include the words: "I am called"?)

Being called is a frightening thing. To think that God would call, choose, and desire to use me for His glory means I've been given an assignment that is way beyond me. What if I fail? I have already—many times. But it's not about me; it's about Him (see v. 31).

I am honored; I am humbled. I remember what I was when I was called. I was not wise by human standards, influential, or of noble birth. But God chose me, called me, and will use me today if I will obey. By His grace, I will.

JANUARY 12

> Though the fig tree does not bud and there are no grapes on the vines, though the olive crop fails and the fields produce no food, though there are no sheep in the pen and no cattle in the stalls, yet I will rejoice in the LORD, I will be joyful in God my Savior (Habakkuk 3:17-18).

Yet is one of those powerful, three-letter words. The prophet chose not to dwell on circumstances that could fill up the debit side of life's ledger. Times were difficult—no denial of that. Based on the visible, the future was not bright. No one would have blamed him for being depressed when he looked out over the fields, orchards, vineyards, and stock pens. It was not a pretty sight. But Habakkuk was not a Pollyanna. His optimism was realistic. His "yet" was a choice: "I will rejoice in the LORD, I will be joyful in God my Savior"—in spite of everything!

JANUARY 13

The streams of God are filled with water . . . (Psalm 65:9).

The Amazon, Nile, and Mississippi/Missouri River systems are the longest in the world. Not everyone can live along these banks, but every one of us needs sweet, fresh, life-giving water in order to survive. Flowing water is best. The length or breadth of the flow is not as important as it brings life to living things along its route.

I am blessed by the psalmist's declaration: "The streams of God are filled with water . . ." He says there is abundance for all who are thirsty. The river of God carries the life of the Spirit. Jesus said, "'Whoever believes in me, as the Scripture has said, streams of living water will flow from within him.' By this he meant the Spirit . . ." (John 7:38-39). I am blessed to be a blessing. River of God, flow through me!

JANUARY 14

Serve him shoulder to shoulder (Zephaniah 3:9).

Back to back is the best defensive formation for a group of soldiers holding a position, as the enemy cannot sneak up on them from any direction. They are on the ready, their eyes focused straight ahead. The message is, "I've got your back; I've got you covered."

Shoulder to shoulder describes the best offensive formation. The picture is of an army on the move. The past has already been dealt with. This is forward progress. New territory is being taken. No enemy can hide from the victorious advance. The army is moving, shoulder-to-shoulder. It's like a group of people looking for a lost child. The searchers walk shoulder to shoulder across the field or through the underbrush. This is how we are to serve the Lord. We are not on an isolated mission. We are in it together, shoulder-to-shoulder.

JANUARY 15

For our light and momentary troubles are achieving for us an eternal glory that far outweighs them all (2 Corinthians 4:17).

The apostle Paul was not a down-in-the-mouth pessimist, nor was he a starry-eyed optimist. I would describe him as a positive realist. He was not in denial about the difficulties of life. "We are hard pressed on every side, but not crushed; perplexed, but not in despair; persecuted, but not abandoned; struck down, but not destroyed" (v. 8). His comparative ledger contains many similar entries.

When I look at the bottom line on the page, I see the reason for his strength. He tallied up the pluses and minuses of his experiences as a committed follower of Jesus Christ and concluded: "My troubles are light and momentary; the glory of knowing Christ is heavy and eternal. I can't help but win, serving Christ!"

JANUARY 16

He enables me to stand on the heights (Psalm 18:33).

Success has been the downfall of many. People can learn to handle lean times, but few are able to handle prosperity. Failure offers less of a risk than success. For some, doing extremely well is the last step before a stumble.

Scripture speaks of this danger. "Pride goes before destruction, a haughty spirit before a fall" (Proverbs 16:18). "So, if you think you are standing firm, be careful that you don't fall!" (1 Corinthians 10:12). That does not mean I should not seek to do well or succeed. It does mean I need to remember that any true success I enjoy comes from the Lord—and give Him the glory.

When I begin to think I can handle life on my own, I'm setting myself up for disappointment and disaster. To be totally dependent on the Lord ensures that He will help me stand, whether in the valley or on the heights!

JANUARY 17

Return to your fortress, O prisoners of hope . . . (Zechariah 9:12).

I like the sound of these words. In context, they remind me of the suffering of God's people over the centuries, the consequence of their disobedience. Would things ever change? The prophet Zechariah stated that their king would one day come (see v. 9). It would be several hundreds of years before Jesus Christ would ride into Jerusalem as a partial fulfillment of the promise (see Matthew 21:5, and following).

In their long history of faith and failure, it was hope that survived through it all. "Hope springs eternal in the human breast . . ." (Alexander Pope, 1733 Alexander Pope. BrainyQuote.com, Xplore Inc, 2012. http://www.brainyquote.com/quotes/quotes/a/alexanderp163156.html, accessed March 7, 2012.). As prisoners in a foreign land, they were also "prisoners of hope"—waiting for the One who was to come.

I can identify. I will return to my fortress, for I too am a prisoner of hope. "And hope does not disappoint us" (Romans 5:5). I wait for Jesus.

JANUARY 18

It is right for me to feel this way about all of you, since I have you in my heart . . . (Philippians 1:7).

Paul's statements to the Christians in Philippi are inclusive. He refers to "all of you" repeatedly. He addresses his letter to all, says he prays for all of them, shares in God's grace with all of them, longs for all of them, and will continue his ministry with all of them (see chapter one).

Verse seven grabs me. His statement was not an attempt to justify his feelings. Feelings are fickle and totally unreliable. Yet the love Paul felt for this company of believers was neither fickle nor unreliable. He carried them, he wrote, "in my heart." With Christ's love in my heart, I shall have room for and be able to love all in a way that is right.

"Lord, let me love with Your love today. Amen."

JANUARY 19

And David shepherded them with integrity of heart; with skillful hands he led them (Psalm 78:72).

These words that describe David the shepherd-king have made their way into my prayers. I want to have integrity of heart and hands that are skillful. Is it better to have an honest heart and no skills, or have skills but be lacking in truthfulness? It's not either-or; it's both-and. I want a heart that is upright and true. I pray with the psalmist: "Create in me a pure heart, O God, and renew a steadfast spirit within me" (Psalm 51:10).

If I am to influence and lead with certainty and wisdom, I need skills that come from the Lord. Integrity speaks of who I am; skills can be learned, honed, and proven. Integrity comes from spending time with God; skills are developed through applied knowledge. "Show me your ways, O LORD, teach me your paths" (Psalm 25:4).

JANUARY 20

However, God has not allowed him to harm me (Genesis 31:7).

Enemies—plots—threats. I don't have to be paranoid to understand that life is dangerous. I have an enemy intent on destroying my family and me. Job can add his personal story. Jesus informed Peter, "Satan has asked to sift you as wheat" (Luke 22:31). Does the Devil have an agenda for my life? Jesus said he does. "The thief comes only to steal and kill and destroy" (John 10:10). That people may not like me is not the problem. The danger is that there is a predator out there who has me and all others who love the Lord in his sights.

Job passed his greatest test. Jesus assured Peter, "I have prayed for you, that your faith may not fail" (Luke 22:32). Whether one enemy or many, "God has not allowed him to harm me." I shall fear no evil. Praise the Lord.

January 21

Read 1 Thessalonians 5:12-22.

Some people think and work best using lists. I'm like that, and I think the apostle Paul was too. As he concluded his first letter to the Christians in Thessalonica, he included a list of behaviors he felt were important, which can serve as a checklist. I'll take a few minutes today to format the list and put it in my Bible or someplace I will visit each day. It is a good reminder of what I need to be working on:

___ Respect those who work hard with me, are over me, and admonish me (vv. 12-13)

___ Live in peace with each other (v. 13)

___ Warn those who are idle, encourage the timid, help the weak, be patient with everyone (v. 14)

___ Always try to be kind to everyone (v. 15)

___ Be joyful always (v. 16)

___ Pray continually (v. 17)

___ Give thanks in all circumstances (v. 18)

___ Do not put out the Spirit's fire; do not treat prophecies with contempt (v. 19)

January 22

You thought I was altogether like you (Psalm 50:22).

I find this statement by God almost unbelievable. Imagine the audacity of anyone thinking that God was all in all, in total, like him. Incredible! Isaiah said some of God's people entertained the same thought in his day: "You turn things upside down, as if the potter were thought to be like the clay!" (Isaiah 29:16).

But God's exposure of the heart and attitude of the people reveals something far more serious than an absurd comparison. An alternate reading is: "You thought the I AM was altogether like you." Look at it again. God said they thought, "the I AM was . . ." To think God is altogether like me strips Him of His deity. To think "the I AM was . . ." makes the eternal a has-been—no longer alive, present, or God! If He is just like me, I'm lost. Only the I AM can save!

January 23

But they did not listen to him because of their
discouragement . . . (Exodus 6:9).

Discouragement makes it hard to hear what I need to hear, as my thoughts become more and more focused on the negative. Then my emotions follow. In a parallel example, Jesus' disciples went to sleep in the garden of Gethsemane. It is Luke, the physician, who includes the defining reason for their slumber. "When [Jesus] rose from prayer and went back to the disciples, he found them asleep, *exhausted from sorrow*" (Luke 22:45, emphasis mine).

The reason I fail to hear does not mean I'm a rebel at heart. Perhaps I'm just discouraged and exhausted from the heaviness of life. "Lord, touch and lift my heart today. Speak rest to my soul so I may clearly hear Your words of promise and may enter into close fellowship with You—even if it means sharing in Your sufferings. Amen."

January 24

Let me die the death of the righteous, and may my end be
like theirs! (Numbers 23:10).

Benjamin Franklin said, "In this world nothing is certain but death and taxes." The Bible says, "Man is destined to die once, and after that to face judgment" (Hebrews 9:27). Taxes are necessary in order to fund life services in our society. Death is certain prior to our Lord's return, with only two possible exceptions (Enoch, Genesis 5:24; Elijah, 2 Kings 2:11).

If Jesus does not return within my lifetime, I will die. It's not of matter of if, only when. How do I wish to die? From sickness, accident, violent act, martyrdom, war, old age? Those are incidentals, not the answer. The answer is found in today's words: "Let me die the death of the righteous, and may my end be like theirs!" Jesus told Peter "by what death he should glorify God" (John 21:19). So whether I live or die, I want to glorify Him! (See Philippians 1:20).

JANUARY 25

I, Paul, write this greeting in my own hand, which is the distinguishing mark in all my letters. This is how I write (2 Thessalonians 3:17).

Written over twenty centuries ago, this passage by the apostle Paul is especially warming. I know times have changed and technology has changed with them. I remember pre-computer days. Now, we have the Internet along with several options in social networking.

The handwritten note or longer letter has been set aside as being too time consuming. I've found my own penmanship has deteriorated beyond what it was before typewriters and word processors. Paul said he was writing his greeting "in my own hand," the distinguishing feature of all his correspondence. Was it grammatically flawless and visually beautiful? I don't know. But to that Paul adds, "This is how I write."

JANUARY 26

I am forced to restore what I did not steal (Psalm 69:4).

I attended an all-church party as a child where we played a group game with uncooked navy beans. Each participant was given a dozen or so. Holding a few beans in our closed hand, we would go to another person and ask, "Odd or even?" If their guess was incorrect, we got to take their beans and add them to our supply. The object of the game was to end up with the most beans. It was great fun until I put my hand into someone else's as though I were going to take his beans. I didn't, but it looked like I had. Suddenly, someone grabbed my wrist and said, "Put them back." My denial was unpersuasive, and I had to surrender my beans. My folly, yes, but I felt wounded. Like the psalmist, I could have said, "I am forced to restore what I did not steal." Some things are not always as they appear.

JANUARY 27

The one the LORD loves rests between his shoulders
(Deuteronomy 33:12).

Moses pronounced the blessing of God's hug on the tribe of Benjamin. As
I read this phrase, I picture myself as being hugged by God. And it feels
good!

Sometimes words are not enough, so a hug helps, saying more than
words ever could. In my relationship with the Lord, I'm glad His hug is
not a polite but stiff expression. Nor is it a passionate embrace that leaves
me feeling violated or taken advantage of. God's hug is an expression of
His love for me. It is non-threatening, though I may be uncomfortable if
I am not in the habit of expressing love in this manner.

Look at the passage again. "The one the LORD loves . . ." That would
be me. I love Him because He first loved me (1 John 4:19). I want to
accept His expressions of love for me. Trusting Him, I "rest between His
shoulders." What a blessing!

JANUARY 28

Who think that godliness is a means to financial gain. But
godliness with contentment is great gain (1 Timothy 6:5-6).

It is a tragic fact that there are those who merchandise the gospel. They
traffic in the things of God merely for their own profit. Jesus drove the
moneychangers out of the temple, saying, "How dare you turn my Father's
house into a market?" (John 2:16). Peter warned of false prophets who
"in their greed . . . exploit you with stories they have made up" (2 Peter
2:3). Paul condemned those who make godliness a charade for the sake of
financial gain. They may have the words and appearance of legitimacy, but
greed is their motivation.

Paul wanted Timothy to know great gain can be acquired when
godliness is lived with contentment. Today is a good day to check my
motives again.

JANUARY 29

Take off your sandals, for the place where you are standing
is holy (Joshua 5:15).

Moses was told to remove his sandals as he stood before the burning bush
(Exodus 3:5). Joshua was told to do the same thing, forty-some years later,
as he stood near the ancient city of Jericho. No burning bush this time,
but the place was still holy. *Place* is not limited to a locality with an address
or two hundred square feet of real estate. *Place* can refer to a number of
things: position, status, opportunity, or responsibility.

Am I aware of the presence of God in my life today? Perhaps this
command serves as a reminder. Wherever I am, whatever my opportunity,
and no matter my responsibility, as a believer, this is a holy moment,
a holy place. I need to take off the reminders of my earthly walk (my
sandals) and listen, worship, and obey. This "place" is holy.

JANUARY 30

Wine that gladdens the heart of man, oil to make his face
shine, and bread that sustains his heart (Psalm 104:15).

This verse describes God's provision for my needs. Wine serves as an
intoxicant, stimulating feelings of wellbeing and joy, and is known for its
celebratory applications. The wine of the Spirit has no negative side effects,
is safe for daily consumption, and fills my heart with the joy of the Lord.
The oil of the Spirit adds the glow of God's presence to my countenance,
speaking of God's anointing that sets me free to minister with winsomeness
and effectiveness. And bread, so ordinary and commonplace compared to
the other blessings, speaks of all that is essential to daily life. Jesus taught
us to pray, "Give us today our daily bread" (Matthew 6:11).

God has provided joy, anointing, and sustenance for me today. I am
blessed!

January 31

I know whom I have believed, and am convinced that he is able to guard what I have entrusted to him for that day (2 Timothy 1:12).

The apostle Paul held a conviction that produced absolute certainty in his life despite the difficulties and suffering he endured. He had someone he could trust completely; someone to whom he could entrust anything and everything that impacted his life. There was no fear of betrayal, no concern of incompetence. All was safe once in the hands of the One who had won his confidence.

The relationship was totally secure, better than any insurance plan. Embarrassment was not a possibility; he would never be humiliated by the decision he had made. Jesus was the one who guaranteed the safekeeping of his sacred trust for time and eternity. I can trust Him too—completely!

February 1

If the LORD is with us, why has all this happened to us? (Judges 6:13).

I have asked this same question. I know the Lord is with me. That being true, I find it hard to come up with an answer to "Why?" when things swirl out of control, leaving me dizzy and confused. Some would add to my suffering by suggesting my difficulty is proof the Lord has abandoned or forgotten me. Or perhaps He is too busy helping others with needs much more important than mine? Some go so far as to question whether professing to belong to the Lord makes any difference at all.

It's that old question: Why do bad things happen to good people? I have no goodness in myself, but I do know I've been redeemed by the blood of Jesus and that His Holy Spirit lives within me. There is an answer to the harassing question, but I just don't have it right now. It's an opportunity to trust Him.

FEBRUARY 2

If I have done any of these, I will make it right (1 Samuel 12:3).

Restitution is an important part of repentance. My greatest debt can never be repaid (Jesus paid it all!), so all else must be offered. One of the best ways to clear the air, as well as offenses, is to follow confession with the offer to make things right. Different wording fits different situations, but one thing is for sure: Don't say it if you don't mean it! Sometimes I've put it in the form of a question: "What can I do to make it right?"

The offended are not always after my blood. A simple, sincere apology may be all it takes. But it may take more. I've never had anyone ask for something totally unreasonable, but if they did, I would go as far as I felt I could and let the rest go. It is easier to work with a person who says, "If I have done any of these, I will make it right." And God's grace is available—every time.

FEBRUARY 3

He sent forth his word and healed them . . . (Psalm 107:20).

Words come infused with power. Every word has significance to it, even the smallest ones. Rolling off the tip of my tongue or pen, words have power to bring life or death (Proverbs 18:21).

The psalmist speaks of the word that was sent to heal. Jesus Christ was the ultimate fulfillment of that statement (John 1:1, 4, 14). He is the living, incarnate Word sent by the Father to bring healing to sin-ravaged, broken, bleeding lives. He came to bring salvation (John 3:17). When He speaks, things happen. The centurion knew that. "Speak the word only, and my servant shall be healed" (Matthew 8:8). Jesus did, and his servant was (v. 13).

Perhaps I could send a word or two today that would encourage faith and bring hope to someone in need. After all, Christ lives in me and His Spirit can direct my words.

FEBRUARY 4

He too shared in their humanity . . . Because he himself suffered when he was tempted, he is able to help those who are being tempted (Hebrews 2:14, 18).

There is nothing sinful about being human. It is the description of how we were made, not an excuse for bad behavior. Here is a wonder among wonders: Jesus shared in our humanity. He was without sin yet truly human.

My humanity has been tainted, warped, and defiled by sin, but that is no reflection on Jesus. He was given the humanity God intended me to have. I suffer as a result of Adam's sin, yet I have no one to blame, for apart from original sin, I have sinned as a result of my own disobedience (Romans 3:23). Jesus came totally free of sin, yet being human, He knows what it is to suffer under temptation's assault.

Jesus is my champion in time of temptation, for although tempted, He did not fail! He will help.

FEBRUARY 5

The king and all the people with him arrived at their destination exhausted. And there he refreshed himself (2 Samuel 16:14).

The people moved at a pace that would normally leave them excessively tired. *Exhausted* is the word. When they arrived at their destination, it was time for refreshment.

Not all journeys are taken at a leisurely gait. Some days you march with quickened step. Other days it seems you've made no progress. Life is not a sprint; it is a forced march. I may not be able to see the finish line, yet I must keep pushing on as if I could. Ziba, Mephibosheth's steward, met David with provisions, among them, "wine . . . to refresh those who become exhausted in the desert" (2 Samuel 16:2).

I'm glad there is the wine of the Holy Spirit to refresh my soul when I'm exhausted from my journey. I will rest today—tomorrow I will press on!

FEBRUARY 6

I waited patiently for the LORD . . . (Psalm 40:1).

I, too, wait, but not always patiently. More often I personify the statement, "I want patience, and I want it *right now!*"

Why is waiting so difficult? Waiting for the unpleasant is called dread. Waiting to get my work done is called procrastination. Waiting beyond my sense of timing is called impatience. Waiting for a promised blessing is called anticipation. Waiting for change is called discontent.

So what is waiting for the Lord? It depends on whether it is something unpleasant, a deadline, something outside my comfort zone, an area I'm unwilling to change, or something wonderful. I can wait patiently if I'm convinced the outcome is well worth the wait. The better I know the Lord, the more I love Him, the more I take Him at His Word, the more I can trust Him with the timing.

FEBRUARY 7

The LORD raised up . . . an adversary . . . And God raised up . . . another adversary . . . (1 Kings 11:14, 23).

Just what I need: another adversary! Isn't life tough enough without adding another enemy? It was God who raised the antagonist in this case. And not just one—two!

It is best to read these verses in context. Solomon had proven unfaithful to God by taking heathen wives in direct violation of His command (v. 2). Those women turned Solomon's heart toward foreign gods, setting him up for God's displeasure and heavy hand; thus, the adversaries. God did it because He loved Solomon.

I can expect adversaries when I live in willful disobedience. If necessary, God may use extreme means in His pursuit of my wayward heart. He does it because He loves me. Will I return to the Lord before He needs to raise "another adversary"? The Prodigal Son eventually got it right (Luke 15:17-20). Will I?

FEBRUARY 8

The sufferings of Christ and the glories that would follow
(1 Peter 1:11).

There are times I find myself messing with God's order of things. I take it upon myself to serve as editor of His holy Word, putting a spin on what He has said in order to serve my own preferences. Dangerous practice! No wonder I end up feeling dizzy and confused.

I must not tamper with truth, especially when I find it uncomfortable to my way of thinking. In this verse, Peter tells me what to expect as a devoted follower of Christ. There is a divine order here: suffering first, and then glory. My flesh prefers there would be no suffering at all, only glory. But that is not the way it was for Christ. Should I expect anything different? Can I really know Christ apart from suffering? (See Philippians 3:10). Paul wrote, "But if we are to share his glory, we must also share his suffering" (Romans 8:17 NTL). There is grace for His way.

FEBRUARY 9

Praise be to the Lord, to God our Savior, who daily bears our
burdens (Psalm 68:19).

Blessings and burdens; my life has had its share of both. They hold each other in balance, and I'm grateful. Here's the best part: the Lord is involved in both.

I like the KJV of this verse: "Blessed be the Lord, who daily loadeth us with benefits . . ." This suggests that the benefits or blessings are so large that they become a burden so heavy that we require help in carrying them. Isn't that neat?

And then there are the things I put in the category of "burden." They are the things that weigh me down, sapping my strength, leaving me exhausted. But the Lord comes to my aid and offers to carry them for me (1 Peter 5:7).

How often can I expect the Lord to help and bless me? *Daily*! After all, it was Jesus who taught us to pray, "Give us each day our daily bread" (Luke 11:3). Blessings and burdens—for these I have Jesus *daily*.

FEBRUARY 10

This is an easy thing in the eyes of the LORD . . . (2 Kings 3:18).

Nothing is too hard for the Lord (Jeremiah 32:17). "Which is easier: to say, 'Your sins are forgiven,' or to say, 'Get up and walk'?" (Matthew 9:5). There is no level of difficulty known to Him. Elisha the prophet spoke: "This is what the LORD says: 'You will see neither wind nor rain, yet this valley will be filled with water, and you, your cattle, and your other animals will drink. This is an easy thing in the eyes of the LORD . . .'" (1 Kings 3:17-18). I like that! My problems pose no problem for Him.

But the supernatural work of God does not excuse me from faith expressed by my obedience. They are what make me a participant and partner in what He is doing. "Make this valley full of ditches" (v. 16). The miracle is an easy thing in the eyes of the Lord, but I still have to dig the ditches.

FEBRUARY 11

Watch out that you do not lose what you have worked for,
but that you may be rewarded (2 John 1:8).

It would be tragic to work long and hard only to learn I had lost what I had worked to make mine. All of those hours would be lost. My best explanations would change nothing. Reconstructing the project may be impossible. The deadline has passed, or someone else has taken my work. Perhaps the fruit of my labor is floating irretrievably in cyberspace. There may be a severe reprimand, but no compensation. I've lost it all. It is even more tragic if I had been warned.

It is most tragic if my loss is in the area of my spiritual life, my life for and with God. The Enemy of my soul is intent upon causing me to lose my reward. Through subtlety and guile, I can be tricked, duped, and hoodwinked. I must be more watchful. Watch and pray!

FEBRUARY 12

All my fountains are in you (Psalm 87:7).

My financial resources are limited. I do not have a large, diversified portfolio. But I have all I need. In fact, I have more than enough. During the economic recession, through years of retirement, even if there should be a repeat of the Great Depression, I'm going to be okay. And here's why. I know my source. (That *s* should be capitalized, by the way.) The Lord is the fountainhead of my life. He is my Source.

I need not depend on the amount or size of my resources as long as I stay connected to *the* Source. This does not give me license to be financially or materially foolish, but it does provide unequaled security. "The LORD is my shepherd, I shall not be in want" (Psalm 23:1). All of my dreams, beginnings, processes, and results will be satisfying as long as they have their source in Him!

FEBRUARY 13

The ministry of prophesying, accompanied by harps, lyres, and cymbals (1 Chronicles 25:1).

The Bible describes spiritual activity I've not personally experienced and have only observed from a distance. This verse describes one such activity that David considered a valid and valuable part of the worship experience. It was provided by a handpicked group of men whose ministry was to prophesy while accompanied by musical instruments.

It seems music can stir up the gift of prophecy. In churches I've been part of, the music stops once an utterance gift begins. Why? The Bible does not require that in all cases. These men prophesied while *accompanied* by harps, lyres, and cymbals. Sounds New Age to us, but it was God's way then. I've heard prophecies sung while accompanied by a group of musicians playing in the Spirit. Amazing . . . and beautiful!

FEBRUARY 14

For the Lamb at the center of the throne will be their shepherd;
he will lead them to springs of living water. And God will
wipe away every tear from their eyes (Revelation 7:17).

The Lamb of God came as the sacrifice for my sin. Spotless, innocent, vulnerable, and gentle, He was the perfect offering in my place. He suffered, bled, and died—for me. He was the lamb who would serve as my shepherd: the "Good Shepherd" (John 10:11), the "Great Shepherd" (Hebrews 13:20), and the "Chief Shepherd" (1 Peter 5:4). He is the one who sits at the right hand of the Father, ever living to make intercession for me. And here He is seen occupying the royal throne, not as the King of Beasts—a lion—but as the lamb. "The Lord *is* my shepherd" (Psalm 23:1, emphasis mine). His loving care will continue throughout eternity. I will follow the Shepherd wherever He leads.

FEBRUARY 15

I run in the path of your commands, for you have set my
heart free (Psalm 119:32).

He has set my heart free. The bondage has been broken. I have been loosed from the entanglements that restrained me. My heart—my inner being—has been set free.

The proof of my freedom is not in my taking license to do as I please; that only leads to further bondage. The proof is in my following the path set by His holy commands. Yes, there are boundaries and restrictions. There are fences and guardrails. But these are in place to protect me. The chains are gone from my heart, but the fences are still there. The fences are not there to keep me in so much as they are there to keep the Enemy out.

I am free to run, to love, and to serve Him. That is liberty of the sweetest kind. "Loving God means keeping his commandments, and really, that isn't difficult" (1 John 5:3 MSG). I'm free! (John 8:36).

February 16

He did not seek help from the LORD, but only from the physicians (2 Chronicles 16:12).

The Bible does not say I must not see a doctor or go to the hospital. It does not forbid me to take medicine or seek treatment for my physical needs. Even though Jesus demonstrated the will of God to heal the sick, He did not chastise the sick and diseased who sought help for their physical malady.

I am not immune to sickness and disease by virtue of being a child of God. I still live in a human body that has not been set free from the consequences of sin. King Asa suffered with a disease in his feet. His disease was severe, and he needed help, but even in his illness "he did not seek help from the LORD, but only from the physicians." My first course of action is to cry out to the Lord and, after that, avail myself of the aspirin, a visit to the clinic, or a 911 call if needed. But I go to the Lord first.

February 17

This sickness will not end in death (John 11:4).

Once I hear a friend or family member has been diagnosed with a terminal condition, my natural thought is, "Oh, no . . . this is it. This is the end." And unless they experience supernatural intervention, those individuals do eventually die of the sickness or disease.

When Jesus heard the news that His friend Lazarus was sick, His response was, "This sickness will not end in death." But Lazarus died anyway. But Jesus never said Lazarus wouldn't die. He said his death was not terminal; it was not the end.

Jesus' words bring comfort and hope to all who know and love Him. Death does not have the final say. Many godly people suffer and die. I am comforted to know they live on with Christ. Death was not the end for them. In Christ we have eternal life! (John 3:16).

FEBRUARY 18

He who sacrifices thank offerings honors me, and he prepares the way so that I may show him the salvation of God (Psalm 50:23).

There is surrender in sacrifice, so my sacrifice involves giving up something I value. My involvement is required. I don't always feel like giving thanks, so to do so anyway costs me something—my feelings. "Let us continually offer to God a sacrifice of praise—the fruit of lips that confess his name" (Hebrews 13:15). Just because my praise is not spontaneous does not mean it is sacrilegious. I offer a *sacrifice*. I surrender my negativity or numbness. I choose to do what is right, regardless of how I feel.

I will begin on my own if need be in order to get in the flow of the Spirit. My sacrifice honors Him and prepares me to receive recovery, deliverance, and further revelation of His love for me. Praise the Lord!

FEBRUARY 19

Then everyone who trembled at the words of the God of Israel gathered around me . . . (Ezra 9:4).

Many people read the Word rapidly without taking time to really "hear" it. I've been guilty of that. Then there have been times when I've *really* heard it, and it has made me shake in my boots!

The Psalms cannot be my sole diet. They are so good, and I can relate to many of them, both in complaint and praise. But there's much more to the Bible than the book of Psalms, and I need it all—even those parts that make me tremble.

To fear God is a good thing. It doesn't necessarily mean I've done something wrong or that my heart isn't right. It may mean I have a healthy, reverential respect for the wonder, power, and holiness of God, who I love. I want people around me who tremble at the Word of the Lord!

FEBRUARY 20

He was a man of integrity and feared God more than most men do (Nehemiah 7:2).

After the walls of Jerusalem had been rebuilt, Nehemiah put his brother Hanani ("my grace, my mercy"[1]) in charge of governing the city and Hananiah ("grace, mercy, gift of the Lord"[2]) was made guardian of the fortress. Together they were made guardians of the newly rebuilt wall.

What Nehemiah found most attractive and desirable about Hananiah was "he was a man of integrity and feared God more than most men do." We could not want a better person in charge of our national security, our churches, our businesses, or our homes. Integrity begins with the fear of the Lord. I want Nehemiah's statement to be true of me.

FEBRUARY 21

Afraid yet filled with joy . . . (Matthew 28:8).

I am fascinated by these contradictory words. How can one be "afraid yet filled with joy"? Was it that what the two Mary's had experienced at the empty tomb was too wonderful for words? The angel had said, "Do not be afraid, for I know that you are looking for Jesus, who was crucified. He is not here; he has risen, just as he said. Come and see the place where he lay." (Matthew 28:5-6) Their hearts were filled to the point of bursting. Were they afraid that if they left this wondrous place and returned they might find the tomb yet sealed, the experience only the fruit of their wishful thinking?

I've been like that at times. Staggered by the reality of His promise, I've allowed fear to hold me back. Today I will go with the joy! I will not be disappointed. The miraculous is real, for Jesus is alive!

---

[1] *Hitchcock's Bible Names Dictionary*, late 1800s, public domain
[2] Ibid

FEBRUARY 22

In your name I will hope, for your name is good (Psalm 52:9).

I have been disappointed when someone has promised something that raised my hopes, but they failed to follow through. Perhaps the promise was beyond what they were able to perform, perhaps they forgot, or perhaps the promise was only words.

I'm sure others have been disappointed in me as well. In some cases, my intentions were good, but my performance wasn't. I have a long way to go before I'm all I want to be when it comes to matching my actions to my words and good intentions. But there is hope for me and for all those like me.

The psalmist had a reliable source. So do I. The Lord is as good as His name, and His name is good. There is nothing about His name He can't fulfill. Trusting Him makes my hope secure. His name is good, and I have hope!

FEBRUARY 23

True wisdom has two sides (Job 11:6).

These words of Zophar, one of Job's friends, open my mind to the possibility that what I have taken for granted may be but part of the whole truth. Years ago, I heard a Bible teacher say, "All truth is parallel." No one statement says it all; there are two sides to every story. You've heard her side, but don't rush to a conclusion until you have heard his side, and vice-versa.

There are two sides to every coin, two possible outcomes. There must be both a positive and a negative charge before there can be a completed circuit. Without both, there would be no action or movement in the universe. My study of the Bible may reveal parallel truths that differ from but complement each other.

Two sides are needed for balance. There is no conflict or contradiction. I need both in order to have light and truth.

FEBRUARY 24

The memory of the righteous will be a blessing . . . (Proverbs 10:7).

Certain names bring back specific memories. Chuck was my best friend during grade school. Alvin was my high school friend who intrigued me with his knowledge of electronics. He and I spent hours working on things for my guitar, recording, car sound system, and so forth. So whenever I hear the name Alvin, I think of him, where he lived, his quiet personality, the kind of car he drove, what we did together—a list of memories I have of him as my friend.

Other names bring back less than happy memories: a class bully, for example. There are names that bring back warm, wonderful memories of men and women whose lives helped and blessed me over the years. I want to be the kind of person Solomon wrote about: the memory of whom is a blessing.

FEBRUARY 25

Each according to his ability, decided to provide help . . . (Acts 11:29).

Many times I've felt bad I haven't been able to do more or give more when appeals have been made for finances or service. If only my desires were matched by my performance. But this statement in Acts gives me reassurance. The Christian brothers living in Judea were in need as a result of a massive famine affecting the entire Roman world. The disciples wanted to help, so they did, each according to his ability. No one was required to do more. As it turned out, the amounts were different, but the sacrifice was the same.

I am willing to give generously, even sacrificially, though it may not be the same amount of finances or time others are able to give. I cannot give what is not mine to give. My ability is not the same, but Jesus said I can give as I have received—*freely* (Matthew 10:8).

FEBRUARY 26

I will awaken the dawn (Psalm 57:8).

David was a morning person. He enjoyed the freshness of the air, the first songs of the birds, and the first rays of the rising sun. I picture his smile as he stretched his arms over his head and said, "Praise you, Lord."

There's nothing like the early morning to get a day off to a great start: a cup of hot coffee, a quiet house, the eastern horizon getting brighter and brighter, a simple greeting to the Lord, and uninterrupted time to read from the Word. I love it! Those are precious times when it's just the Lord and me. Should I oversleep, get distracted, and miss the dawn, I feel like I have lost an important part of my day.

I need my time with the Lord every day, and for me, morning is the best time. I will be a morning person. "I will awaken the dawn."

FEBRUARY 27

The wise heart will know the proper time and procedure.
For there is a proper time and procedure for every matter . . .
(Ecclesiastes 8:5-6).

It is frustrating when one is trying to get a project completed and nothing fits. The pieces are scrambled, and deadlines are approaching. I don't enjoy those situations. My head aches, and my palms sweat. *I'm going to be late, I just know it,* runs through my mind.

I need to remember to seek the Lord. Nothing needs to be left to chance. He has promised wisdom to those who ask Him (James 1:5). I can move forward with a sense of timing and knowledge of how to proceed. Gone is the reason to be frustrated or anxious. There is assurance for a good outcome. Could there be a better way to serve the Lord? I don't think so. There is a right way and a right time. "Lord, give me the wisdom that lets you be Lord of my work and time."

FEBRUARY 28

Be joyful in hope, patient in affliction, faithful in prayer
(Romans 12:12).

The modifying words are especially interesting to me. "Joyful in hope"
describes the effect hope has upon me. It sets me free from anxious care
and fills my heart with joy. It changes my entire outlook on my life.

"Patient in affliction" is a goal. It is not a natural response to be patient
while suffering affliction. Without doubt, patience is what I need. This
identifies an area where I need the grace of God in order to experience the
kind of strength that holds me steady when the difficulties of life come.

"Faithful in prayer" is my daily assignment. It is my part, something
I can choose to do. It requires discipline as well as diligence. It is my
call to obedience. If I am faithful in prayer, I will be given patience in
my afflictions and the joyful assurance that in Christ I have hope. I can't
lose!

FEBRUARY 29

The tongue that brings healing is a tree of life . . . (Proverbs
15:4).

The "tree of life" is first mentioned in Genesis (2:9; 3:22, 24) as being in
the middle of the garden of Eden. The last place you find this tree in the
Bible is in the book of Revelation where it is mentioned four times in two
chapters (Revelation 2:7; 22:2, 14, 19). In each case, it is preceded by the
definite article, *the*.

Apart from Genesis and Revelation, "tree of life" is found four other
places in the Bible, and all in the book of Proverbs (3:18; 11:30; 13:12;
15:4). There, however, it is preceded by an indefinite article, *a*. Obviously,
Solomon was not writing of the same tree, yet he saw parallels. Proverbs
18:21 says, "The tongue has the power of life and death . . ."

Which tree is growing in my mouth? Do I bring life or death by what
I say?

MARCH 1

If you do not stand firm in your faith, you will not stand at
all (Isaiah 7:9).

I believe many things but not all equally so. Some are based on my own
intellect and reasoning. When I say, "I believe," I may only mean that
I'm thinking something may be so, i.e., "I believe March will have better
weather than February." Based on past statistics or experiences, I still don't
know if March will be stormy or fair.

My faith—what I live by—must be more than mere belief and not
left to hearsay or past experience. My faith must be correct and current.
Orthodoxy of thought alone will not hold me steady. What I believe about
life, God, and myself must become convictions worthy of life and death.

My faith must be built on God's Word. If I hold tenaciously to those
tenets of righteousness, I will stand. If not, I will not stand at all. Today,
I will stand!

MARCH 2

May he give you the desire of your heart and make all your
plans succeed (Psalm 20:4).

"Dear friend, I pray that you may enjoy good health and that all may go well
with you, even as your soul is getting along well" (3 John 2). Both verses
sound like wishes, but these expressions are not sloppy sentimentality.
They were desires expressed to God on behalf of another. In John's prayer,
the good health and all going well were based on the recipient's healthy
relationship with God. David's psalm expresses the same relationship.

Success is not determined by my getting what I want; it's the outcome
of my getting what God wants: "May *he* give you the desire of your
heart . . ." (emphasis mine). How can I know what He wants for me?
"Delight yourself in the LORD and he will give you the desires of your
heart" (Psalm 37:4). As I delight, He gives the desires. I will delight in
Him today!

MARCH 3

Expressing spiritual truths in spiritual words (1 Corinthians 2:13).

There is a reason for the blank looks and silent responses when we talk to some people about the things of God. It isn't that they are rude; they just don't get it. They don't understand what we say. You would think they could understand their native tongue. They can, but what they hear is not what is being said. "Born again," "justified," "repentance," "faith"—and on and on. It doesn't register.

Even though the words are recognized, they are not understood. Strange? Not at all. People in their natural state cannot understand the spiritual meaning embodied in God's Word. Even Jesus' disciples did not understand many of the things He said to them. The words they knew; the meanings they did not. The Holy Spirit enables us to discern the language of heaven. Teach me more today.

MARCH 4

If you have raced with men on foot and they have worn you out, how can you compete with horses? (Jeremiah 12:5).

One difficulty has followed another. I have struggled in prayer with decisions I've needed to make, my attitude, health issues, family concerns, and more. There have been no quick answers. And then, I have experienced a reassurance through the Word that brought a measure of relief. I've been able to move forward a step or two. Ah, at last. But no, it is not the last. There will be something else, often more severe and longer lasting.

I'm tired of this relentless cycle: struggle, pain, questions, prayer, waiting—and waiting some more. But there is a reason. God said, "If you have raced with men on foot and they have worn you out, how can you compete with horses?" He's getting me ready to compete with horses!

MARCH 5

She did not consider her future (Lamentations 1:9).

This phrase explains the fatal flaw of Jerusalem. Chosen and blessed of God, she became careless and then contaminated. Willful sin hastened her decline. The blessing she once knew ceased to flow. She had been shamed and finally ignored by those who once held her in awe.

There were early signs of danger that should have caused her to turn back to the Lord, but "she did not consider her future." She assumed life would continue as she had enjoyed it. Sin changed that, and she was left to mourn her loss. Had she considered her future, she would have realized sin was leading to her ruin. She was in danger of losing it all. The trade was not worth it. Without the blessing, the future was bleak.

There is much I can learn from Jerusalem's sad experience. I will consider my future and stay close to the Lord.

MARCH 6

For he grants sleep to those he loves (Psalm 127:2).

Those who are able to sleep well at night should consider themselves profoundly blessed—and I do! If I lie awake, I try to determine if there is something the Lord wants me to hear or pray about. If nothing comes in a few minutes, it is back to sleep for me.

The context of Solomon's lyrics, however, is about those who "in vain . . . rise early and stay up late, toiling for food to eat." (v. 2) He wrote that such toil is both futile and unnecessary.

The times are difficult and may become more so, but God takes care of His own. Work is honorable, but worry, dread, and anxious care are not. A marginal note in my Bible offers this alternative reading: "For while they sleep, he provides for those he loves." Praise the Lord for His loving care! I can rest peacefully, knowing He will provide all that is needed!

MARCH 7

I boasted . . . about you, and you have not embarrassed me (2 Corinthians 7:14).

It is a wonderful thing to know people you don't have to worry about embarrassing you. It's not that I expect perfection out of any of my friends and loved ones. I just enjoy bragging about those who have done well, have achieved certain goals, and have lived lives worthy of emulation.

Genuine compliments are affirmations of one's relationship. I may speak freely about certain ones because they are "the real deal"—neither plastic dolls nor cardboard cutouts. I am not embarrassed to have my name associated with theirs for they have proven what they're made of. How wonderful when the comments made are about their life and service for the Lord!

I have been honored to know many people who are glowing examples of lives lived for God's glory. May the Lord bless you, one and all!

MARCH 8

Those who prophesy out of their own imagination . . . (Ezekiel 13:2).

Counterfeits would not exist if it were not for the genuine article. That is as true in the supernatural realm as in the natural. There are prophets, and there are false prophets. The difference is in the spirit that inspires them. The fact that false prophets exist should encourage us to know the Holy Spirit prompts God's people to speak His messages. There must be the real before there can be the counterfeit.

But here is a prophet of a different sort: A person who prophesies out of his or her own imagination. Prompted by their own thoughts and desires, they say what they want to be true. What is said may not be evil or untrue; it's just not God's truth for this particular time. Passed off as a word from the Lord, it seeks to justify itself without the validation of the Holy Spirit. Danger lurks. Prophets beware!

MARCH 9

Renounce your sins by doing what is right . . . (Daniel 4:27).

How can I know I have properly dealt with my sins? I must repent. How do I do that? I must agree with the evidence as revealed by the Bible and the Holy Spirit that I am wrong and have done wrong. That's confession. I must feel my sorrow, not just say the words. That's godly sorrow (2 Corinthians 7:9-10). I must change the way I think about my sin and do an about-face in my behavior.

How am I or anyone else going to know that I am truly sorry and have repented? I demonstrate true repentance when I change the way I think about my sin, renounce it, and change my behavior by doing what is right.

Repentance begins in my heart and mind but gives observable evidence in how I live.

MARCH 10

You let men ride over our heads; we went through fire and water, but you brought us to a place of abundance (Psalm 66:12).

David knew the emotion accompanying betrayal, the dangers of being a fugitive, the physical deprivation of being away from home and provision, the torment of the unknown, the pain of personal failure, and more. But in those times, all he needed to do was remember the goodness of the Lord he knew and trusted, and his heart was lifted, his spirit revived.

God's people could recite their history complete with danger, struggle, failure, and victory. But the final chapter was always one of hope. Disobedience had brought much of their pain, but some of their suffering had been the result of God's work—testing, disciplining, and refining them in order to bring them to "a place of abundance."

God is at work in my life also, and His desire for me is the same: *abundance* (see John 10:10). Lead on, Lord!

MARCH 11

Whatever happens, conduct yourselves in a manner worthy
of the gospel of Christ (Philippians 1:27).

The word *whatever* covers a lot of territory. I'm going to use the phrase "no matter what" as a synonym. It removes every exception. Nothing is excluded. It encompasses all of life, and life includes the good, the bad, and the ugly.

"Whatever"—no matter what happens, Paul writes, there is a divine directive to be followed. There is a code of conduct that supplies the answer for how I am to behave. I am to conduct myself "in a manner worthy of the gospel of Christ." I am to respond to life and the people in it in a way that will draw people to Christ rather than drive them away from Him. I am to give evidence of the grace of God that enables me to endure hardship and overcome opposition with a healthy, holy attitude.

My life is to show the difference Christ has made in me. Does it?

MARCH 12

Woe to those who plan iniquity, to those who plot evil on
their beds! At morning's light they carry it out because it is
in their power to do it (Micah 2:1).

When asked why he had committed moral indiscretion, a former US president responded with, "Because I knew I could." Power, prestige, and opportunity do not give permission for unacceptable behavior. Some people take what does not belong to them, indulge in risky practices, take advantage of children and vulnerable adults, and drive over the centerline of life in ways that make even the society fringe shudder. When confronted or exposed, their explanation for their audacious impudence has no more substance than "because I knew I could."

Are my excuses any different? Where is the fear of God in all of this? I need to "love the LORD [my] God, walk in all his ways, obey his commands, be faithful to him, and serve Him with all [my] heart and all [my] soul" (Joshua 22:5 KJV).

MARCH 13

The LORD your God is with you, he is mighty to save. He
will take great delight in you, he will quiet you with his love,
he will rejoice over you with singing (Zephaniah 3:17).

Picture the heavenly Father relating to His children. He stays close to them,
bending over to protect them. He smiles when He looks at them, bragging on
them at every opportunity. Imagine He has their pictures on His refrigerator
door. (I like that!) When His children are fearful, sick, or whiney because of
their weariness or discomfort, He soothes and comforts them, speaking in soft
and loving tones, reassuring them that He loves them. As they lay exhausted in
His arms or stir restlessly in their sleep, He croons over them, sometimes with
songs they know, at other times with songs known only in heaven.

We teach our children to sing, "Jesus loves me, this I know." And He
does!

MARCH 14

Unless the LORD had given me help, I would soon have dwelt
in the silence of death. When I said, "My foot is slipping,"
your love, O LORD, supported me. When anxiety was great
within me, your consolation brought joy to my soul (Psalm
94:17-19).

I am just going to ruminate on these words today without any programmed
prompting. This is one of those many passages in God's Word where
commentary is not required. I'll just sit here and soak in the warmth of
His love. I'll let the memories of specific times He helped me flow through
my mind and heart. I'll prayerfully respond if His Holy Spirit reminds me
of areas where I still need His help. I may even sing my praises if it seems
that is the best way to express my love to Him in these special moments.

The reality of my situation and the truth of His Word meet in my
daily meditation. It is good to spend time with Him!

MARCH 15

Therefore encourage each other with these words (1 Thessalonians 4:18).

There is no message more encouraging for days like these than that it won't be long before we will "meet the Lord in the air. And so we will be with the Lord forever" (v. 17).

I dread turning on the television. It's just more graphic pictures and descriptive audio about murder, deception, scandal, lies, natural disaster, violence, threats, betrayal, immorality, blasphemy, uncertainty, promises, denials, and on and on. And that's just the nightly news! The entertainment is ribald, story themes are marbled with provocative behavior, language is loaded with innuendo, and the most private subjects are openly discussed on the talk shows and replayed again and again on the commercials. Love and marriage are ridiculed and replaced by sleazy sexuality. I'm sick of it.

Be encouraged . . . Jesus is coming!

MARCH 16

The flock detested me, and I grew weary of them . . . (Zechariah 11:8).

I smiled as I read this passage. The identities parallel that of a congregation (the flock) and its pastor (the shepherd). Strained relationships can develop between the two.

I love the honesty of God's Word. No sugarcoating here. Most pastors love their parishioners, and congregants love their pastor, but wherever people are involved, it is only a matter of time before emotions get out of balance. Hurting people hurt people, and our present-day churches are full of hurting people.

Moses had difficulty with the people he was trying to lead—something like trying to herd cats. And it was more than just a bad day that prompted Zechariah to write the above passage

Sheep/people, shepherds/pastors. I'm glad Jesus is the Good Shepherd! I want to be more like Him.

MARCH 17

Before he had finished praying . . . (Genesis 24:15).

God is not locked into one way of answering my prayers. I would like Him to always answer in a timely fashion—like right now! And sometimes He does. At other times, He calls me to a season of prayer, which may last a period of weeks, months, or even years, mixed with faith and patience. How wonderful when, after waiting in prayer for an extended period of time, He suddenly answers, taking me by surprise.

When I demand God to answer on my time schedule, I limit myself to how I can experience the wonder of His variety and wisdom. Abraham sent his servant on a trip to find a wife for his son. The outcome had to be right. The servant prayed, not knowing how long he would have to wait. And then . . . (I like this!) "before he had finished praying," God answered.

MARCH 18

Misuse your name (Psalm 139:20).

The Ten Commandments make it explicitly clear: "Thou shalt not take the name of the Lord thy God in vain" (Exodus 20:7 KJV). As a child, I got the idea that meant it was wrong to cuss, or use profanity, so I was very careful not to do that and felt uncomfortable when I heard others "take the name of the Lord in vain." I still do.

One day, conviction settled over me while I read the words in another version of the Bible. Instead of being limited to cussing, I learned the meaning is to *misuse* His name; to make it of no effect; to waste its power by treating it as trivial or common; to minimize its holiness through casual use; to attach it to my agenda or interpretation with no regard to His will or character. And I've been guilty of those things! "Lord, help me to reverence Your name!"

MARCH 19

The Lord will rescue me from every evil attack and will bring me safely to his heavenly kingdom. To him be glory for ever and ever. Amen (2 Timothy 4:18).

It is no secret that I am a target for the enemies of God. Satan and his evil horde are against anyone who loves the Lord and wants to do His will. Satan is a deceiver, a liar from the beginning, formidable in his power, and heinous in his activities. Just speaking of him sends a cold chill down my spine. I need not live in fear of him, however, because the One who is in me is "greater than the one who is in the world" (1 John 4:4).

I'm no match against my adversary in my own strength. I am as a lamb among wolves, yet I need fear no evil, for the Lord is with me. It is He who "will rescue me from every evil attack and will bring me safely to his heavenly kingdom." To Jesus be the glory both now and forever. Amen!

MARCH 20

In your unfailing love, you will lead the people you have redeemed (Exodus 15:13).

God has made a life-changing, eternal investment in me. He established my worth through the price He paid for me in the death of His Son. I am redeemed—bought back! I am twice His. He loved me before He redeemed me, has loved me ever since, and always will love me.

Such love is beyond explanation but not beyond experience. It is unfailing, certain, trustworthy, unshakable, consistent, and enduring. Every act of God toward me comes out of that love. I can trust Him today and always. He will never lead me astray nor subject me to any unnecessary experience.

So where will He lead me today? I may not know specifically, but I don't have to. It is enough to know, "He guides me in paths of righteousness for his name's sake" (Psalm 23:3). In that, He is honored, and I am blessed!

MARCH 21

But the people grew impatient on the way . . . (Numbers 21:4).

I'm in good company. It is comforting to know there are others who grow impatient. It's not that we're always impatient. If the airplane is on time, dinner guests are not late, problems are solved within the hour (like they are on television), and answers come as soon as the question arises, I'm good. I'm patient—always! But I can grow impatient if the above-mentioned situations and hundreds like them are not taken care of in a timely way. Yes, I'm in good company.

But if I read the statement in context, I see I'm *not* in good company! Read on: "They spoke against God and against Moses . . . Then the LORD sent venomous snakes among them; they bit the people and many . . . died" (vv. 5-6). God is not pleased when my impatience leads to speaking against Him or my spiritual leaders. It is sin.

MARCH 22

You stoop down to make me great (Psalm 18:35).

What a picture: God bending over and stooping down to make me great! How does any of that make sense?

God doesn't have to make sense when it comes to my understanding. What I consider wise is foolishness to Him, and His ways are past my ability to understand. But this statement absolutely baffles me. God on His knees for my benefit! The New Testament picture of this is of Jesus kneeling in front of His disciples with a towel and basin to wash their feet.

How does His stooping down make me great? Jesus modeled true greatness. He said, "The greatest among you will be your servant. For whoever exalts himself will be humbled, and whoever humbles himself will be exalted" (Matthew 23:11-12). Jesus stooped down so that I could become great by following His example.

MARCH 23

But encourage one another daily . . . (Hebrews 3:13).

There's nothing like a word of encouragement to provide a lift. I don't even have to be feeling low before I can be blessed by it. It's like walking down the street of life and having someone on the sidewalk cheer as I go by.

A word of encouragement identifies those who support me. They push me forward in the right direction. I am not alone. Someone believes in me. I am heartened, and my spirits are raised.

I know how much a word of encouragement means to me, but are others affected the same way when I cheer them on? I'm sure they are. We are to "encourage one another daily." Apparently that's not too often. Rather than trying to think of someone who is so low they need encouraging, I should assume everyone could use a positive word . . . today!

MARCH 24

A freewill offering in proportion to the blessings the LORD your God has given you (Deuteronomy 16:10).

Some religious events are announced as being on a freewill offering basis. That means there is no charge. All are welcome to attend and give a financial contribution if they wish, which reminds me of "love offerings"—same idea, different terminology. Sounds warmer and gentler, but the actual count at the close of the service is often more "love" than "offering." The guest(s) would be sent down the road with a check for a token amount and feeling less loved to boot.

God set the parameter for the freewill offering to be in proportion to the blessings received. I know when my heart has been touched and my life blessed through someone's ministry, I want to give more than if I had purchased a ticket.

MARCH 25

You are very old, and there are still very large areas of land to
be taken over (Joshua 13:1).

I wonder how Joshua felt hearing God say he was old—and not just old,
but *very old*. I might joke about my age, but I'll do it on my terms. I've
been more sensitive about my age depending on where I was in life. As
a child, I didn't want to hear I was too young if it meant I was not old
enough to participate in or enjoy what was reserved for the more mature.
On the other end of life, I don't want to be told I'm too old to hold a job
I enjoy or be overlooked because someone younger is preferred. Yet I must
remember that a stated fact is not necessarily an insult. I think it rather
amusing that the Lord, the Ancient of Days, told Joshua, "You are very
old." Not old compared to God, for God is ageless.

My age is just a fact of my life. It is not time to quit; great challenges
lie ahead. I must go on!

MARCH 26

You turned my wailing into dancing; you removed my
sackcloth and clothed me with joy, that my heart may sing
to you and not be silent (Psalm 30:11-12).

I'm not sure I know how to wail, but I do know what it is to cry and to
moan. There have even been a few times in my life when I have screamed.
But wail?

I've heard the sound of wailing. It is a bone-chilling howl, often an
expression of pain, grief, or fear, and has an animal-like timbre, such as
when wolves and dogs bay at the moon. I've seen video clips of people in
the midst of disastrous situations, wailing over the loss of loved ones.

David had experienced the transforming power of God's grace, turning
his "wailing into dancing" and his sorrow into joy. My broken heart can
sing again because of Jesus.

MARCH 27

To this you were called . . . to this you were called (1 Peter 2:21; 3:9).

God's people have a sense of having been called. I've been called out of darkness into His wonderful light (1 Peter 2:9). But suffering is part of this calling. It is to this I was called because Christ suffered for me and in that left me an example I should follow (2:21). While going through the suffering that accompanies persecution, I am not to repay evil with evil or insult with insult. Instead, I am to bless those who persecute me, because to this I was called (3:9).

Having been called to suffer, I have been given the privilege of knowing Christ in the fellowship of His sufferings (Philippians 3:10). I have been called to exemplify the words of Jesus in the Sermon on the Mount (Matthew 5:44). His life made a difference for me. To this I am called for His glory!

MARCH 28

I will sift them for you . . . (Judges 7:4).

It is possible to have too many volunteers or too many options. Too many volunteers may result in people tripping over one another, impeding progress. Too many ideas or options may result in confusion because of the clutter that distracts or blurs one's focus.

I may try to sort things out for myself, not all of which is bad. But what if I include things or people who prove to be detrimental in terms of the desired outcome? When personalities or strategies interfere with what God wants to do, I may not be the one who does the separating. I am intrigued that God said He would do the sifting. He is not pruning; He is sifting. He is not cutting back; He is separating out.

It is best to let the Lord do the sifting, for even if it appears I end up with less, I will win greater victories. Less is more!

MARCH 29

He has hidden himself among the baggage (1 Samuel 10:22).

The moment of truth had come: Young Saul had been anointed privately by the prophet Samuel to serve as king over Israel. Now it was time for the public announcement. But when the people went looking for him, Saul was not to be found. But God knew where he was—"hidden . . . among the baggage."

I wonder how many others have tried to hide themselves among their "stuff" (KJV)? We all bring a certain amount of baggage with us on our journey of life. When God calls us to serve Him in a specific way, we may try to hide among our baggage. The stuff we have accumulated in our lives, whether possessions we have amassed or hurts we have saved up, is nothing but added baggage when it comes to serving the Lord with total freedom.

God knows when I'm trying to hide among my stuff.

MARCH 30

Blessed are those who have learned to acclaim you . . . (Psalm 89:15).

True praise is something that can be learned as a result of instruction, observation, and practice. I may venture a simple, "Thank you, Lord." That's a start, and I may expand on that by repeating the phrase or adding others to it. But there is more for me to learn. I must learn to "acclaim" Him.

Acclaim means, among other things, to "applaud." I know how to do that. I applaud someone for a good effort, for a task well done, or because I liked what I saw or heard. I've even heard of giving the Lord a "clap offering" during a service, which is a step up from the rest. But the psalmist was talking about something more than a courteous clapping of the hands. He was talking about thunderous, enthusiastic applause, a standing ovation. Such praise pleases the Lord—and I am blessed!

MARCH 31

To enable us to serve him without fear in holiness and righteousness before him all our days (Luke 1:74-75).

Aged Zechariah and his barren wife, Elizabeth, had just become the parents of John, later known as John the Baptist. The Holy Spirit filled the once-mute Zechariah, and he began to prophesy that his son would be the one who would go on before and prepare the way of the Lord (v. 76).

God had kept His promise regarding the coming Christ, and Zechariah enjoyed a double blessing: news that his niece Mary was to be the mother of the Lord and the birth of his own son in his old age. Both births were an act of Jehovah God. It was all too wonderful for words—yet Zechariah's words flowed.

As with Zechariah, the fulfillment of God's Word make it possible for us to serve Him without fear. And so I am able to serve Him today . . . because God came near!

APRIL 1

The weapons of war have perished! (2 Samuel 1:27).

Saul and his son Jonathan fell in battle while fighting the Philistines. David, himself a fugitive, heard the tragic news and raised the pitiful lament three times, "How the mighty have fallen!" (1:19, 25, 27). The third time, however, he added, "The weapons of war have perished!" He was not speaking about swords, spears, or arrows sped to their targets by powerful bows. He was speaking about the men themselves, especially those who were in leadership positions.

The people of God are "the weapons of war." They are the ones God uses to contain, drive back, and destroy the evil that slinks, lurks, taunts, attacks, imprisons, and takes the lives of men, women, and children. When spiritual leaders fall, morally or from fatigue in spiritual battle, we lose some of the weapons of war so desperately needed in the battle!

APRIL 2

And this thing became a sin . . . (1 Kings 12:30).

Some things are not a sin themselves. Gold is not a sin by nature. An ornament in the shape of a calf is not a sin. A calf made out of gold is not a sin. Having more than one calf made of gold is not a sin. But this thing became a sin because of *why* it was made and *how* it was used. Gideon made a sacred ephod of gold, which Israel worshipped, and it "became a snare to Gideon and his family" (Judges 8:27).

There may be things in my life that are innocent and acceptable in their own right. But if they are misused, abused, or given more importance than they deserve, they can become a sin in my life. "Search me, O God, and know my heart; test me and know my anxious thoughts. See if there is any offensive way in me, and lead me in the way everlasting" (Psalm 139:23-24).

APRIL 3

The LORD confides in those who fear him; he makes his covenant known to them (Psalm 25:14).

I love the words the Holy Spirit chooses in order to reveal God's truth. As in this case, I learn that the Lord shares things with some people that He does not share with others, much like a circle of friends to whom He offers privileged information, intentionally kept from the general public. He keeps it not because it is a guarded secret, but because it is only for those who are in loving relationship with Him. They are those who fear him with the holy reverence He deserves, so He shares the secrets of His heart and the wonders of His covenant with them.

I picture Him coming near and leaning over to whisper His promises into the ears of His people. I desire that closeness with Him and to hear His voice today!

APRIL 4

> Don't be afraid . . . Those who are with us are more than those who are with them (2 Kings 6:16).

I need to get past things as they appear to my human eyes and intellect. Too often, I judge outcomes according to the obstacles perceived by my eyes or negatives conjured up by my mind. But that is not the accurate view, as my natural perception is not dependable. I can call what I see "facts," but if I allow them to control my faith in a negative way, it's because my set of facts is off the wrong list. Faith is based on fact, but the criterion is what God has said in His Word.

I need not fear if I take my eyes off the Enemy's horde and onto the heavenly host. I am not alone. I may be surrounded and feel overwhelmed, but if I ask the Lord to open my spiritual eyes, I will discover there are more for me than against me.

APRIL 5

> And with him will be his called, chosen, and faithful followers (Revelation 17:14).

Those who will accompany the King of Kings and the Lord of Lords in apocalyptic warfare are clearly identified, and their descriptive adjectives are given in ascending order: 1. They are "called." The call to come to the Master includes all, the "whosoever" (John 3:16); 2. They are "chosen." The reality, however, is that "many are called, but few are chosen" (Matthew 22:14). They become chosen when they hear the call and respond in faith (1 Peter 2:9); and 3. They are "faithful." Their faithfulness is proven through obedience and endurance. They are authentic, reliable, and most wonderful of all they are *His*.

"Lord, I want to be in that number—called, chosen, and faithful!"

APRIL 6

Be strong and courageous, and do the work . . . (1 Chronicles 28:20).

David instructed his son Solomon to be strong and courageous because building the temple would not be an easy task. He would need inner resolve to carry the load that would accompany the assignment.

Whatever lies before me today will require that I be strong and courageous. Life isn't easy. It calls for the best that is within me, and each day requires strength and courage. I must give attention to the condition of my health, physically, mentally, emotionally, and spiritually, and that requires focus and discipline. But I must also do the work. I can't shut myself off from the practical aspects of everyday life.

As a believer, every area of my life is sacred. I must be strong and courageous, yes, but I must not forget to do the work the Lord has set before me. Now to work . . .

APRIL 7

You have punished us less than our sins have deserved . . . (Ezra 9:13).

Maturity has a mellowing effect upon people, if they let it. I haven't mellowed out in every area of my life and am shocked at my immaturity. God and I will continue to work on those areas together.

I have noticed some improvement, however. For example, many times when I was a child, I thought I was being treated too severely for my misbehavior. My mother made me stand in a corner or sit on a chair. My father used his razor strap on me—smooth side as well as rough. I often protested with tears, saying the infraction wasn't my fault, I didn't mean to do it, or whatever else I could come up with to try to lessen or escape my punishment. But now that I'm older, I realize that I have been punished less than my sins have deserved. That's called mercy.

"I'm thankful for Your mercy, Lord!"

April 8

Read Psalm 34.

The setting is 1 Samuel 21. David fled for his life, as King Saul was determined to kill him. Questioned by Ahimelech, priest at Nob, David resorted to lying about why he was alone, without provisions or weapons. He might have pulled off the ruse, but Doeg the Edomite, Saul's head shepherd, was there and saw him, so word was surely going to get back to King Saul.

David continued his flight to Gath, where Achish was king. Achish's servants recognized David and brought his identity to the king's attention. Terrified, David pretended to be insane, scratching on the doors and letting his saliva run down his beard. Achish was repulsed. "Look at the man! He is insane!" (1 Samuel 21:14).

But Psalm 34 proves that David was not insane; fearful, yes, but not insane. Fear makes one do things that do not please the Lord. Psalm 34 promotes sanity. I need to read it again and rejoice.

April 9

They knew he was talking about them (Matthew 21:45).

When a huddled group of people is speaking in low tones while looking in my direction, I just *know* they are talking about me. My imagination kicks in as I try to figure out what they are saying. It generally is not a positive moment, emotionally.

Jesus did not have to point His finger or call someone by name before they got the message that He was talking about them. And they knew why. Conviction accompanied the truth as Jesus spoke.

I too have been in those settings, such as while listening to a sermon or sitting at home reading my Bible, where I've gotten the distinct impression that He's talking about me. And I too knew why. But it was not always a negative thing. Sometimes I've "heard" the truth of His promises and knew: He's talking about me!

Whether conviction or confirmation, I want to respond appropriately.

APRIL 10

The people worked with all their heart (Nehemiah 4:6).

Nehemiah was blessed to have people who worked alongside him with all their heart. The task of rebuilding a wall, which would have been impossible with half-hearted effort, became possible as everyone did their part—and did it with all their heart. This is one way we demonstrate our love for God.

The first and great commandment is that I love the Lord my God with all my heart, soul, mind, and strength. The second is to love my neighbor as myself (Mark 12:30-31). These two commandments are comprehensive in their scope and powerful in their expression. As I work with others for the glory of God, we will accomplish more and demonstrate what it means to love God. To do it with all my heart speaks of attitude, desire, and effort. No shortcuts here!

APRIL 11

In all this, Job did not sin by charging God with wrongdoing (Job 1:22).

It is easy to get out of line with my thoughts and speech. I grumble, complain, criticize, and blame. And that's just in my conversations with God! How many times have I sinned through what I've said or thought? But must I be so careful in how I talk to the Lord? Isn't He big enough to hold up under my ranting and raving?

Job had reason to question, complain, rant, rave, and blame. After enjoying such a wonderful relationship with God, he was bereaved of family and suffered financial loss. Would he not be justified in holding God accountable, in condemning God for how He protects or cares for those who love Him? Yet, "in all this, Job did not sin by charging God with wrongdoing." I have much to learn from Job's example. With David, I will pray (Psalm 19: 14).

APRIL 12

May people ever pray for him and bless him all day long (Psalm 72:15).

It's easy to find fault with leadership. No one can satisfy my demands all the time. No one can "get it right" every day. If I'm looking for a reason to criticize, I'll be able to make a list as long as my arm. But what if I were to pray for those in leadership? Would things change? Maybe not—but I would. My heart would soften, my attitude would become more positive, my expectations more realistic, and my outlook more hopeful.

Praying for leadership is between God and me. *Blessing* leadership is between my family, friends, associates, and me. The prayers I offer for leadership may be private, but the blessings and other positive statements should be public.

Private praying keeps public commendation honest and sincere. Would things change? I believe as people change, things can change.

APRIL 13

And the power of the Lord was present for him to heal the sick (Luke 5:17).

This statement is fascinating. It also raises some questions: Was the power to heal not always present? Was this a special anointing? One day He did not do many miracles because of the unbelief of the people (Mark 13:58). Other days He performed miracles in spite of an unbelieving crowd (Matthew 12:9-13). Sometimes Jesus healed all the sick present (Matthew 12:15). Other times it was only one out of a larger group. Yet all He touched and all who touched Him in faith were healed.

When we pray for everyone, all may not be healed. There are reasons for this. Would we have more successful outcomes if we were led by the Spirit as Jesus was? On this particular occasion, the power of the Lord was present for Him to heal the sick. There are times of special anointing. Perhaps this was one of them.

APRIL 14

An anxious heart weighs a man down, but a kind word
cheers him up (Proverbs 12:25).

Life can get unbearably heavy at times. The world has become an
unfriendly place for the human race. Directly and indirectly, we all contend
with inadequate income, health issues, political unrest, interpersonal
relationships, questions of faith, and uncertain futures. We are filled with
apprehension, a nervous uneasiness in the pit of our stomachs, and a
relentless parade of troubling thoughts. We've become obese as we seek
to medicate our worry by gorging ourselves with food. But the weight
we have added to our bodies does not compare to the burden anxiety has
added to our souls.

We are self-centered and self-indulgent—and it hurts our family,
friends, and us. We're disgusted with the way we look and feel. Perhaps a
kind word would help. It's the least we can do.

APRIL 15

When the sentence for a crime is not quickly carried out,
the hearts of the people are filled with schemes to do wrong
(Ecclesiastes 8:11).

We like to think we are the most civilized nation on the planet, as we work
for a gentler, kinder world. Tolerance is given a higher moral ranking than
the Judeo-Christian teaching of justice and righteousness. Holiness of the
heart has been replaced by political correctness. There are many opinions
when it comes to the subject of capital punishment, which doesn't seem the
right course of action for a civilized people—though we have little problem
with the extermination of persons before their birth, thus preventing their
potential talents from being added to a needy world. Laws are made but
not enforced. Tough talk only results in tough lawbreakers.

Justice delayed speeds us on our way to a lawless society. Righteousness
will strengthen a nation.

APRIL 16

Know that the LORD is God. It is he who made us, and not
we ourselves (Psalm 100:3).

Benjamin Franklin has been called America's original self-made man,
which means he went far beyond what his original circumstances indicated
was possible. Abraham Lincoln was another, as he came out of obscurity,
overcame obstacles of every kind, and rose to prominence and influence
by willpower and hard work.

To say someone is a self-made man or woman is meant to be a
commendation of the highest order. But I do not want to be a self-made
man. I want to be a God-made man. What I may accomplish along my
journey will be the result of God's grace at work in my life. He alone
knows my full potential. My efforts are inadequate, but I can do all He
wants me to do through Christ who gives me the strength (Philippians
4:13).

APRIL 17

Then Nathanael declared, "Rabbi, you are the Son of God;
you are the King of Israel" (John 1:49).

These words sound similar to Peter's confession in Matthew 16:16. There
is an important difference, however. While Nathanael's declaration came
in the opening days of Jesus' ministry and Peter's much later, Jesus gave
more spiritual credence to Peter's than Nathanael's. Apparently Nathanael's
statement was not something Jesus could build His church on, as it was
based on his own deduction. Peter's declaration was the result of divine
revelation.

Man's conclusions, even if they contain true statements, do not
generate a living faith. Only that which comes to us out of an authentic
relationship with Christ has life.

APRIL 18

In that day the LORD will whistle for flies . . . and for bees . . .
(Isaiah 7:18).

Of all the things I can picture God doing, this is probably the last on a long, long list. Roy Rogers used to whistle for his horse, Trigger. Anyone with a dog knows how useful it can be to whistle for it to come. I don't know if you can whistle for a cat or not. But whistle for flies and bees? It strikes me as laughable.

Some versions of this verse use the word *hiss*, a sound of derision and scorn, rather than *whisper*. To whistle is to summon with a shrill sound.

Without referring to the context in which this verse appears, I'll leave this thought: God is capable of communicating with all of His creation. When He summons, His creatures respond. Where He sends, they go. Of all the creatures on Earth, only human beings ignore and disobey Him.

APRIL 19

He did what was right and just, so all went well with him. He defended the cause of the poor and needy, and so all went well. Is that not what it means to know me? (Jeremiah 22:15-16).

If my life isn't changed in the most fundamental ways, I don't know God, regardless of what I say. The secret of King Josiah's successful reign is attributed to his relationship with the Lord. Yet his special relationship was not in areas totally unattainable to any of the other kings who reigned. Things went well with King Josiah, God said, because he "did what was right and just," and "defended the cause of the poor and needy." If I turn the question into a declarative sentence, God said, "That is what it means to know me."

Is my relationship with God couched only in religious lingo, or is it demonstrated in daily living? Do what is right in His eyes, and all will go well!

APRIL 20

Arrogant, overfed, and unconcerned . . . (Ezekiel 16:49).

I am surprised these words are used to describe Sodom, as I generally think of the open homosexuality practiced in that ancient city (Genesis 18:20; 19:4-5). (*Sodomy* takes its name from the city of Sodom.) But these three words in Ezekiel aren't nearly as "bad" or obviously wrong. Are they? I am startled that God would say, "Now this was the sin of your sister Sodom . . ." (v. 49).

There is an uncomfortable similarity to our own times—even apart from the gay lifestyle. I could use synonyms to describe some of the citizens of my city—prideful, obese, and apathetic—and am shocked at how closely they come to describing *me* some days!

I must repent of all expressions of pride, lack of control, and a careless attitude. These sins contributed to the downfall of Sodom, but sin can be forgiven!

APRIL 21

When I awake, I am still with you (Psalm 139:18).

It was a long night that started with difficulty in falling asleep. Activities of the day flooded my memories. Conversations repeated themselves in my inner ear. My weary body tossed and turned and finally collapsed into a state of unconsciousness where wild things chased me through my dreams until the alarm clock called me to rise. It was then I learned something I had not been aware of earlier. I had not been alone. The holy presence of my Lord had lingered by my bedside watching, listening, protecting, and loving me through the dark night hours. And when I fully awoke, rubbing the sleep from my eyes, I discovered He was still there.

I was amazed at how refreshed I felt. My mind was clear, my body rested. I greeted Him with a whispered praise and rose to live this new day.

APRIL 22

I do not have, but what I have I give you (Acts 3:6).

If I made a list of what I perceive to be my strengths, it would turn out to be a short one. If I listed what I see as my weaknesses, it would be a much longer list. But would those lists be completely accurate? In my mind, they would be. Were I standing beside Peter and John in Acts 3, I could come up with a lengthy list of what I do not have, including such things as social skills, appearance, soaring confidence, impressive abilities, and on and on. That's why we need each other. If we help each other, it will be amazing what we can accomplish together.

Peter didn't have it all either. He did not have what the lame man wanted—silver and gold—but he did have what the man needed—Jesus.

Rather than bemoaning what I don't have, I will give people what I do have. I'll give them Jesus!

APRIL 23

Daniel spoke to him with wisdom and tact (Daniel 2:14).

Wisdom and tact are two traits absolutely essential in the life of a Christian. The greater the possible outcomes, the more care must be exercised in how things are said and ideas presented.

Wisdom goes beyond knowledge. Wisdom has to do with how and when knowledge is applied. Perception and insight walk hand-in-hand through the dialogue process. Tact is the partner that seizes the right moment by acting in a winsome, convincing, and effective manner. Wisdom does the deep, inner work; tact guides the outer, public presentation.

Together, wisdom and tact navigate dangerous waters and delicate topics, bringing new life, fresh ideas, or closure as needed. When in the life of a believer, they become the means the Holy Spirit uses to bring hope and resolution to difficult situations.

APRIL 24

And what does the LORD require of you? To act justly and to love mercy and to walk humbly with your God (Micah 6:8).

Pleasing God is not all that difficult, but there are prerequisites. Those obligations are not left up to my whim or spur of the moment inspiration. They are set by God himself.

But there is no mystery here. God is not into guessing games. What He desires, what He requires of His people, is clearly spelled out and revealed so that I might move ahead in obedience to His will.

God's expectations and requirements are perfectly attainable by those who love Him. "Act justly," with fairness and integrity; "love mercy," and extend it to others; and "walk humbly," with modesty and respect, "with [my] God." I will do that.

APRIL 25

Who despises the day of small things? (Zechariah 4:10).

I find it easy to view things as too small to be used or too insignificant to matter. I'm always looking for bigger ideas, more substantial resources, and greater talent. First efforts may seem to be too little, too weak, or too whatever to be successful. But have I forgotten the size of an atom? In grade school, I learned it was the smallest building block of matter. But that information has been outdated by more recent discoveries of quarks and leptons, which exist inside of atoms, and scientists believe there may be something even smaller. How amazing!

The Creator has revealed that He delights in using small things to build His universe. And He uses small communities, small churches, and insignificant people to build for eternity. Little is much when God is in it. Be in me, O Lord!

APRIL 26

Though I walk in the midst of trouble, you preserve my life; you stretch out your hand against the anger of my foes, with your right hand you save me. The LORD will fulfill his purpose for me; your love, o LORD, endures forever (Psalm 138:7-8).

The Lord is actively involved in my life today. There is no detail that escapes His notice, no need that misses His attentive care, no cry of my heart that He does not hear. He is the Savior of every area of my life, spiritually, mentally, physically, and emotionally.

God's overshadowing intent is this: He loves me and will fulfill His purpose for me, which is to glorify Him. What an honor! He takes the rough materials of my life and blends them together in such a way that the good He intends will emerge. All I need do is love Him with all my heart, soul, mind, and strength. I can trust Him for the rest.

APRIL 27

I urge you . . . to join me in my struggle by praying to God for me (Romans 15:30).

Prayer is a way we can join one another in the struggles of life. It may not be possible for me to be present physically, to offer a listening ear or a shoulder to lean on, but I can stand by you in prayer. I may be aware of enough details to pray from a knowledgeable position, or I may not know anything about what you're going through other than what the Holy Spirit has brought to mind, prompting me to pray for you. Sometimes the nudge is more like a shove; the need is urgent, no time to dally. I may awaken in the middle of the night with your face before me or your burden pressing upon me.

What a privilege to know I can join you in your struggle by praying to God for you. And there may be times the Holy Spirit may prompt you to pray for me. What a blessing to know we can pray for each other!

APRIL 28

I will not leave you until I have done what I have promised
you (Genesis 28:15).

Is God in a hurry? Is He in such demand by needs greater than mine that
He can't afford to finish what He started? Am I in danger of having Him
called away by someone else's cry or a global emergency? Not according to
this text. When God makes a promise, it is a binding commitment on His
part; a covenant. Elsewhere, the Bible records this confirmation: "And I
am sure that God, who began the good work within you, will continue his
work until it is finally finished on that day when Christ Jesus comes back
again" (Philippians 1:6 NLT).

What a way to live! He has promised to make me more like Jesus,
and He won't leave until He has accomplished that good work. "Lord, I
don't want to sabotage what You are doing through foolish disobedience
or unbelief on my part!"

APRIL 29

Select capable men . . . men who fear God, trustworthy
men . . . appoint them . . . Have them serve as judges for the
people . . . If you do this and God so commands, you will
be able to stand the strain, and all these people will go home
satisfied (Exodus 18:21-23).

Just because a pastor is doing the work of the kingdom does not make the
work any easier. Anyone in leadership can tell you that wherever people
are involved there will be issues, situations, and challenges of all sorts.

Moses was born and groomed for leadership. Early on, he made a
flawed decision that cost him greatly. Later, he led his people but was
overwhelmed by the load he tried to carry. His father-in-law wisely advised
him on what to do in order to stand the strain. Moses followed the advice,
and the people went home satisfied.

APRIL 30

O Sovereign LORD, my strong deliverer, who shields my
head in the day of battle (Psalm 140:7).

There are many things you can lose in battle yet still survive, but your
head is not one of them! And it is amazing what the human body can lose
yet continue to function. Loss of limb curtails movement and dexterity.
Loss of sight removes perspective and plunges one into darkness. Loss of
hearing muffles sounds and may result in living in total silence. Yet despite
these losses, a person can live a meaningful life. But he or she must *not* lose
his or her head!

When David struck down Goliath, he cut off the giant's head, and
that was the end of him. David knew the danger of battle and put his
trust in the LORD, his strong deliverer, who shielded his head in the day
of battle.

I've been given the helmet of salvation and more (Ephesians 6:13-17).
I must keep my head in battle!

MAY 1

Your path is a reckless one before me (Numbers 22:32).

Childhood is marked by imaginary friends and creative play and youth by
impulsive decisions and carefree behavior. Much of this is a normal part
of growing up. Recklessness, however, is not limited to any particular age.
You might consider a person's age, but the tragedy mounts as the individual
grows older. As the saying goes, there is no fool like an old fool.

In the above passage, the angel of the Lord spoke directly to Balaam a
chilling statement that carried a frightful warning. Balaam was in danger
of severe consequences. God has given us His Word to instruct us because
He knows and understands our tendency to be rash in speech and behavior.
Recklessness puts us in harm's way and in danger of God's displeasure.

I must be careful.

MAY 2

My conscience is clear, but that does not make me innocent
(1 Corinthians 4:4).

Conscience is a beautiful gift from God to every human soul and serves as a first-level alert in times when I'm in danger of violating a basic moral law. It is reliable and strengthened when heeded but is influenced by culture, relationships, and further instruction, which can be a plus or minus, depending on the input I accept.

My conscience can be sharpened or dulled. The Bible says my conscience can be "seared" (1 Timothy 4:2 KJV), leaving it, like a burn scar, without sensitivity. Underdeveloped, incorrectly taught, ignored, or unresponsive, my conscience is not the final word on moral purity. A child may begin innocently, but left to his own ways, he will go astray. I must heed God's Word and Holy Spirit.

MAY 3

The LORD your God . . . turned the curse into a blessing for you, because the LORD your God loves you (Deuteronomy 23:5).

I love this passage. Fortunately, I have not heard all the curses that have been directed at me over the years, but I know there have been some. Some people may not just dislike me, they may disdain, even hate me.

Israel's enemies hired the prophet Balaam to pronounce curses on her, but the Lord "turned the curse into a blessing." Wow! Think of it. God can take the worst people say about me and the darkest curses they pronounce upon me and turn them into blessings! I don't know how many times He has done this for me, and it's probably better that way.

God blesses us because He loves us. Personal curses are turned into personal blessings. What a wonderful Savior!

MAY 4

He was not the only one who died for his sin (Joshua 22:20).

Some people assume their unacceptable behavior is their own business as long as it does not hurt anyone else. Achan may have thought this way when he hid things devoted to the Lord in his tent after the fall of Jericho. But the Lord had said it was all to be destroyed. Achan assumed no one knew about his indiscretion, but he was wrong. God knew. When confronted, Achan confessed and faced the consequences. But "he was not the only one who died for his sin." The consequences were greater than he could have ever imagined. His fellow countrymen died in the battle at Ai, and Achan's sons and daughters joined him in losing their lives as they were stoned to death and their bodies burned.

I must remember: Others may suffer as a result of my sin.

MAY 5

We will not hide them from (our) children; we will tell the next generation the praiseworthy deeds of the LORD, his power, and the wonders he has done (Psalm 78:4).

Sharing my spiritual heritage with my children and grandchildren is a wonderful privilege. Following through on this opportunity takes an intentional decision on my part and quality time, beginning with having a story worth telling.

My relationship with the Lord must be meaningful enough to have resulted in a change in my life. I must take advantage of the day-to-day opportunities in the normal ebb and flow of life, seize the teachable moments they bring, and in a natural way share the supernatural, eternal truths of knowing God. How can I expect my offspring to be excited about living for Him unless I am?

MAY 6

Go in the strength you have . . . (Judges 6:14).

I don't have the strength to do it all, but I do have strength to do something. If I wait until I think I have all the resources I need—the funds, training, time, or connections—I'll never even start, to say nothing of finishing.

But God doesn't expect me to have it all before I begin. His encouragement is to go in the strength I have, and He will provide what more is needed. As long as I stay close to and obey Him, there will be enough strength, resources, funds, training, time, and connections necessary to take the next step.

Let the adventure begin!

MAY 7

But we have this treasure in jars of clay to show that this all-surpassing power is from God and not from us (2 Corinthians 4:7).

Patsy Clairmont wrote a delightful book entitled, *God Uses Cracked Pots* (Tyndale House Publishers, 1999), and some would label Patsy a crackpot. While she does have a ready wit, I must not miss the depth of her message.

One thing can be said about cracked pots: they leak a lot. Is that so bad? Not if what's inside is aromatic or sweet. A sealed container may preserve what's inside, but no one will benefit from its contents until it is broken. The apostle Paul wrote of a treasure residing within us, jars of clay. As the treasure is of God, the jar relates to the clay of our human and often broken vessels.

God is pleased when our "cracked pots" release His power for the benefit of others and the glory of His name.

MAY 8

A boy wearing a linen ephod (1 Samuel 2:18).

At first glance, this description may sound old-world but hardly significant. I would miss an important truth if I were to read past this phrase without pausing to think about it.

Samuel's mother promised to give him to the service of God all the days of his life, so he lived in the temple at Shiloh under the guidance of Eli, the high priest. The linen ephod was a garment originally worn only by the high priest. For Holy Scripture to record "a boy wearing a linen ephod" is extremely significant. To me it says God will use our youth in holy service if they will separate themselves for His glory.

There is no higher calling, no greater honor, than to serve Him!

MAY 9

You have killed those who should not have died and have spared those who should not live (Ezekiel 13:19).

Even lifted out of context, this statement exposes a chilling example of profound injustice. The innocent were executed and those guilty of heinous crimes were set free. What a travesty of moral justice.

I must not justify myself by pointing a finger at the judicial system or making reference to life on the street. I am ashamed to confess that I have been guilty of the same behavior. Not in physical fact but in my mind and heart. John said anyone who hates his brother is a murderer (1 John 3:15). Have I pronounced sentence upon those who have "wronged" me? I'm in no position to pass judgment (Romans 12:19).

MAY 10

In the council of the holy ones God is greatly feared; he is more awesome than all who surround him (Psalm 87:7).

There is no competition in the presence of God. When Lucifer tried to draw attention away from the Almighty and siphon some of the glory for himself, he was immediately removed from his position and expelled from the royal court.

The fear of the Lord causes the heavenly host to tremble not because God is a despot but because He is awesome—"more awesome than all who surround Him." All who abide in His holy presence are overwhelmed by His greatness and humbled and honored to serve Him. Am I left breathless when I consider the Lord in the beauty of His holiness?

MAY 11

Read 2 Samuel 6:12-23, paying particular attention to vv. 12-19 regarding conduct, v. 20 regarding criticism, and v. 23 regarding consequences.

These three points—conduct, criticism, and consequences—serve as a reminder of what is involved in the everyday experiences of life. There will always be those who criticize the behavior of others, even when that conduct is appropriate in the eyes of the Lord.

I must be careful that I do not judge by outward appearances. God doesn't. He looks at the intent of the heart, the motive behind all behavior. David's wife Michal lived a barren life as a result of her criticism of her husband.

Sincerity alone does not make my actions acceptable, but the more my life is lived for the glory of God, the more pleased He will be with me. I put myself in danger of spiritual barrenness when I criticize that or who pleases Him. Change my heart, O God!

MAY 12

The LORD has given him over to the lion . . . (1 Kings 13:26).

I know the story of Daniel in the lion's den, but this story is different, as it is not about one of God's people being delivered out of harm's way. This story is about God *throwing* someone to the lions. A frightening thought! The man of God had disobeyed God's instructions, and God considered it serious enough that He not only allowed a lion to kill him, He *gave* him to the lion.

Peter wrote that the Devil goes about like a roaring lion, looking for someone to devour (1 Peter 5:8). But this case is different. God may use severe means in dealing with His people (See 1 Corinthians 5:5). Sometimes God's grace is expressed through a severe mercy.

MAY 13

Don't be afraid of them. Remember the LORD, who is great and awesome, and fight for your brothers, your sons and your daughters, your wives and your homes (Nehemiah 4:14).

My home and family are in grave danger of assault and battery from this world's system every day. There are threats designed to contaminate, intimidate, and eventually exterminate the virtues and values I ascribe to under God.

Somebody needs to do something, but I can't wait for "somebody" because they might arrive too late. *I* am the one who must fight—and I must fight for my brothers and sisters, my sons and my daughters, my wife (husband), and my home. I must remember the Lord, who blessed me with family, and remember that He cares more about them than I ever could.

Rather than being fearful, I must be faithful and fight in the strength of my great and awesome Lord. We can win!

MAY 14

And he sent a man before them—Joseph, sold as a slave (Psalm 105:17).

I like the thought that someone has gone before me. It may be virgin territory as far as I'm concerned, unknown, uncharted, and unclear. There may be trepidation on my part. I'm uncertain, nervous, a little anxious. But when I see a road or path, a signpost, or even a gum wrapper, I know another human being has been here ahead of me.

So it is with the ways of the Lord. God always has His man or woman to lead the way. Joseph was God's choice. He was sent ahead of his family but getting to his God-appointed place meant he first was sold as a slave.

Difficult, inconvenient, painful experiences may be God's way of getting me where I need to be in order to be a blessing to others. Am I willing, even if it means being sold as a slave?

MAY 15

What has happened to me has really served to advance the gospel (Philippians 1:12).

The apostle Paul did not write about lucky breaks that brought opportunity and spectacular outcomes to his life. He did not write about the reward of hard work or the compounded benefit of cooperative efforts. When I read the story of his life, I learn that he was speaking out of difficult and painful circumstances. His missionary trips were not vacations to exotic places to speak at a couple of conferences and enjoy good food and fancy accommodations. He wrote while buffeted by man and nature, leaving him broken and physically ill. He wrote under threat of death, chained to Roman guards. Yet as he reflected on all he had endured, he wrote, "What has happened to me has really served to advance the gospel."

How is my life serving the cause of Christ?

MAY 16

Jehoahaz sought the LORD's favor, and the LORD listened to him . . . (2 Kings 13:4).

There are many things I might ask the Lord to give me. They might include health in body and relationships, provision of daily needs, the blessing of friends, the addition of material possessions, the recognition of effort expended or service rendered, among others. Can I imagine the Lord would take special notice of such requests or pursuits? Perhaps He would, but that would be up to Him.

Jehoahaz found the sure way to get God's attention: He sought the Lord's favor. Favor suggests acceptance and approval. To me it suggests warmth of relationship that expresses itself in seeking to bring good to the one who receives His attention. This is how I want to live. With His smile of favor upon me, He will listen to my cry.

MAY 17

The people rejoiced at the willing response of their leaders, for they had given freely and wholeheartedly to the Lord. David the king also rejoiced greatly (1 Chronicles 29:9).

Over the years, I have sat in services where appeals to sacrificial giving were made in order to meet some need or to further some project. Those appeals can become pretty intense and emotional. If I feel I am being manipulated emotionally, I stiffen up and keep my hands in my pockets, along with my wallet. On the other hand, when I see my leaders responding enthusiastically and generously, I am stirred to give. I know I may not be able to give the same amount as some of them, but we can all give at the same sacrificial level.

Being genuine in my giving will inspire others to give. God loves a cheerful giver (2 Corinthians 9:7), so I want to give freely and wholeheartedly. I want my King to rejoice greatly!

MAY 18

This is what the Lord says: "Restrain your voice from weeping and your eyes from tears, for your work will be rewarded," declares the Lord. "They will return from the land of the enemy. So there is hope for your future," declares the Lord. "Your children will return to their own land" (Jeremiah 31:16-17).

These words are so powerful I must read them slowly, pause, think about them, and then read them again. Life is filled with tears. Sometimes I wonder if my best work really made a positive difference in the life of my children. But the Lord says yes, my work will be rewarded. Even if it seems my children are held captive by the Enemy of their souls, there is hope.

Hope always relates to the future. The past may be filled with regret, the present with struggle, but there is hope: My children will return. They will come home to me and to the Lord! My voice is lifted in praise to the One who has promised and is at work even now!

MAY 19

I am forgotten by them as though I were dead; I have become like broken pottery (Psalm 31:12).

Some days I feel forgotten, that I might as well be dead. If I died in the next week, for example, people would come to my funeral—perhaps more than I expect, perhaps less. But after the songs, the memories, the words by the pastor, the funeral luncheon, and the graveside committal, I would be forgotten in a matter of time. And that might not take as long as I would hope. Only the ones who loved me most would care. It's just the way life is.

Would it be any better to be like broken pottery, when the pieces of my life outlive their usefulness? To dwell on either scenario is unproductive unless I remember that I have some say in how I live and how I die. May I live and die so that I glorify my Lord. To the degree that is so, my living shall not be in vain!

MAY 20

You will not have to fight this battle. Take up your positions; stand firm and see the deliverance the LORD will give you . . . (2 Chronicles 20:17).

There are so many verses in the Bible that speak of struggle and conflict. Warfare on all fronts is described. The call goes out that I must put on the whole armor of God and fight, fight, fight. I'm battle-weary, exhausted from the constant struggle against evil. As Paul wrote, "No rest but . . . harassed at every turn—conflicts on the outside, fears within" (2 Corinthians 7:5).

Today's verse is especially refreshing in my devotional time with the Lord. At times like these, there is rest in the midst of the battle, for the battle is the Lord's!

MAY 21

Train yourself to be godly (1 Timothy 4:7).

The word *godly* is spelled with a small *g*. There is no suggestion to become divine, as only God is. To be godly is to act in a way that is compatible or in harmony with His nature and speaks of a life that is pleasing to Him.

Godliness, with a small *g* is something that can be learned, but one must be a member of His family before his or her actions are truly in the spirit or character of who He is. If my name were Smith, others outside of my family might do things in a "Smith-y" kind of way, but they would not have the Smith DNA, heritage, or lineage. They would just be going through the motions.

I must train myself to be godly, to find those things within me that come from Him, and discipline myself to express them in ways that come out of the life flow of His Spirit.

MAY 22

You harbored an ancient hostility . . . (Ezekiel 35:5).

I've met people like this. They are burdened with an old grudge or offense. They keep carrying it around, even though they have forgotten what they were so upset about. They can't seem to let the anger go and protect it with a vengeance. They suppose they are getting back at the offender, but the one who originally committed the terrible wrong has long since gotten on with their life.

The inner poison becomes more toxic as the offense is carried, protected, and nurtured. Feelings of rage may surface without provocation, lashing out at whoever is at hand. I've purposed not to let my emotional caldron boil over. Ancient hostilities will make me ancient, old before my time. Whether real or imagined, old hurts are like thunder clouds without life-giving rain. Let them go!

MAY 23

You do not stay angry forever but delight to show mercy (Micah 7:18).

God does not hold a grudge. He has great patience, but there comes a time when He takes action. I really like that He "delight[s] to show mercy." To me that means God takes pleasure in clemency.

It's not that He looks the other way when I do wrong; He sees it all, and my waywardness and disobedience are a direct affront to a holy God. If I got what I deserved, I would suffer greatly or be instantly annihilated. But neither has happened, and not because I'm better than anyone else or He loves me more. It's that He takes pleasure in showing mercy. He withholds the harsh treatment I do deserve and provides the good treatment I don't deserved. Mercy and grace work hand in hand.

MAY 24

He who is pregnant with evil and conceives trouble gives birth to disillusionment (Psalm 7:14).

Then, after desire has conceived, it gives birth to sin; and sin, when it is full-grown, gives birth to death (James 1:15).

There is a striking parallel between these two verses, written over one thousand years apart by two men of God. I don't know if James is quoting David, using different words, or if the Holy Spirit inspired each to write totally independent of the other. Both use colorful, descriptive words to describe a process that starts with desire, continues through conception, and results in disenchantment and death.

My basic desires are not wrong or evil, but they may become so if they are impregnated through wrong choices and behavior. The outcome can only be trouble, sin, and death. Solomon wrote, "Above all else, guard your heart, for it is the wellspring of life" (Proverbs 4:23). That's the secret.

MAY 25

And Judas Iscariot, who became a traitor (Luke 6:16).

I don't believe Judas Iscariot was *predestined* to betray Jesus. That would mean he had absolutely no choice in the matter, damned before he was born. God's divine and perfect foreknowledge sees things that will be done as though they were already done. I often miss the interlock between the two.

Today's verse throws clarifying light on the process. Judas was not a traitor when he was born, though his DNA may have included the proclivity for dishonesty and betrayal. He yielded to his natural bent and became a thief (John 12:6), listened to his misdirected heart, and became a traitor. His fatal sin was not the betrayal of Christ; it was his failure to repent.

An obedient, living faith in Christ lets me become a child of God. Without that, I could become another Judas.

MAY 26

So he said, "These are the two who are anointed to serve the
Lord of all the earth" (Zechariah 4:14).

There is a special action on God's part that prepares His people for
effective service: Anointing. I capitalize the word to indicate it is an action
transcending any taken by human beings. Humans may be involved, as
the prophet Samuel was, who anointed Saul and then David as king of
Israel. The pouring of oil over someone's head doesn't automatically make
them a king of anything, but when that act is carried out in obedience
to a divine command, there is an Anointing imparted that enables and
empowers the recipient to carry out the will of God with effectiveness,
wisdom, and power.

I want God's Anointing upon my life. I want the blessing that helps
me to serve Him in the power of His Holy Spirit. The Anointed life is not
about me; it's all about Him!

MAY 27

The second son he named Ephraim and said, "It is because
God has made me fruitful in the land of my suffering"
(Genesis 41:52).

It is difficult to express much joy when in the midst of suffering. Speaking
for myself, I don't handle suffering well, which is probably why I need to
experience it from time to time. It's too easy to become complacent and
take the blessings of life for granted. Living with that attitude, I would
eventually spoil and become mushy, messy, and good for nothing. Rotten.
So God allows me to suffer. I am grateful that my sufferings have not
stretched over decades, though at times it seemed like an eternity.

Ephraim was born while Joseph was in Egypt, the land of bondage. The
years there had been long, difficult, and filled with suffering. Ephraim's
birth reminds me that I, too, can be fruitful in the land of my suffering.

MAY 28

Then the LORD said to Moses, "I will rain down bread from heaven for you. The people are to go out each day and gather enough for that day. In this way I will test them and see whether they will follow my instructions" (Exodus 16:4).

Some procedures seem so unnecessary. Why, when I go to have a simple medical procedure, do I have to answer the same questions over and over again? What is my name, birth date, telephone number, address, why am I there? I tell them, and then I tell them again. Are they trying to drive me crazy? Do they want to see how long it will take before I break?

I wonder if the children of Israel got tired of going out every day and gathering only enough manna for that day. Did it seem unnecessary when they had containers large enough to hold an entire week's supply? But God was testing them. Would they follow His instructions? Will I?

MAY 29

Egypt was glad when they left, because dread of Israel had fallen on them (Psalm 105:38).

The evacuation (mass departure), or rapture (ecstatic catching away), of the church will bring mixed reactions from those left behind. It will be a terrible moment of truth for those who had heard the gospel and felt the tug of the Holy Spirit's conviction upon their hearts but never got around to putting their faith in Christ and devastating for those who thought they were "okay" but never had the inner witness of the Spirit. For others, it will be party time. Once the initial shock passes, many will be relieved that the "holy antagonists" are finally gone. Good riddance! Now they can get on with life as they want it—free of God and those who said they loved Him.

Our presence is a thorn in this world's flesh, and our absence will be this world's demise. "Even so, come, Lord Jesus!" (Revelation 22:20 KJV).

MAY 30

So that in every way they will make the teaching about God
our Savior attractive (Titus 2:10).

Presentation is what makes a good meal even better. When we go out
to eat, the cleanliness of the facility, the pleasantness of the hostess, the
expertise of the chef, and the attentiveness of the waiter are all part of
our consideration. My spouse and I enjoy the sights, sounds, and aromas
that provide the ambience for our special time out. But unless our food
is presented in a way that speaks of care in preparation and creativity in
appearance, I will probably choose a different restaurant next time. I am
especially disappointed when the finished product is not as attractive as
the picture on the menu.

This is the sort of care I need to take when presenting the gospel,
leading a Bible class, or speaking in ordinary conversation about the Lord.
I must do all I can to make the teaching as attractive as my subject.

MAY 31

For I am going to raise up a shepherd over the land who will
not care for the lost, or seek the young, or heal the injured,
or feed the healthy, but will eat the meat of the choice sheep,
tearing off their hoofs (Zechariah 11:16).

God told Zechariah to take up the equipment of a foolish shepherd (v.
15), as He was going to expose the complacency and selfishness of those
considered spiritual leaders in that day. Everything God said about those
leaders was negative, and He was going to demonstrate their true behavior
despite the religious garb they wore or the spiritual jargon they used.

The reality is God wants to see the opposite of each negative point in
those who lead His people. They must care for the lost, seek the young,
heal the injured, feed the healthy, and protect the wellbeing of all. "The
LORD is my Shepherd; I shall not be in want." (Psalm 23:1)

June 1

The secret things belong to the LORD our God, but the things revealed belong to us and to our children forever, that we may follow all the words of this law (Deuteronomy 29:29).

I don't think it's possible that I can or ever will know everything God knows. That's because He's God and I'm not. Those things are "secrets," withheld not to keep me ignorant but left unknown because of their magnitude in number and glory. Even with a glorified body and all human limitations removed, the enormity of the omniscient, omnipresent, and omnipotent One will never be exhausted by any of His creation.

I'll leave what I can never know with Him and seek to live according to what I can know—those things that have been revealed and will yet unfold throughout eternal ages. God has revealed all I need to know to please Him here.

June 2

But if serving the LORD seems undesirable to you, then choose for yourselves this day whom you will serve . . . But as for me and my household, we will serve the LORD (Joshua 24:15).

Choices are personal and powerful. Others may choose what happens to me, but I retain the privilege and responsibility to choose what happens within me. Some options are more desirable than others, and some choices are easier to make than others. And the outcomes of my choices vary in scope and intensity. It is obvious that some choices are more important than others, but some are more important than I originally thought them to be.

God allows me to make the ultimate decision of my life. I can choose to serve and obey Him, or I can choose to ignore and disobey Him. I will follow Joshua's example and choose to serve the Lord!

JUNE 3

The LORD's right hand has done mighty things! The LORD's right hand is lifted high; the LORD's right hand has done mighty things! (Psalm 118:15-16).

I could be wrong, but it sure sounds to me like the Lord is right-handed. Biblically, the right hand speaks of position, privilege, and power. As to position, it speaks of placement. As to privilege, it speaks of honor. As to power, it speaks of might and strength. If I were left-handed I might feel differently about this, as though I were less like Him than I actually am.

But this isn't about me, it's about Him. Jesus is seated at the right hand of the Father, the place of privilege and authority. And from that position He is praying for me and acting on my behalf. His right hand is lifted high in authority and blessing. He is doing mighty things. All is well!

JUNE 4

And so after waiting patiently, Abraham received what was promised (Hebrews 6:15).

There are years and years of silence in the word *waiting*. The key to the length is found in the word *patiently*. I often find it hard to wait three minutes for the light to change at an intersection. To wait for God to bring about things He planted in my heart months ago is more than I can bear.

Abraham waited years, and the Scriptures say he waited patiently. But the waiting was longer than that; it was *after* waiting patiently that he received. Obviously, I'm too impatient. I blow my horn in the microsecond between the light's changing from red to green. I drive away rather than wait five more minutes for the store to open at its posted time. I suspect many times I've given up just short of receiving God's provision. Abraham is the father of all those who by faith wait. I want to be like him.

JUNE 5

The LORD said to Gideon, "You have too many men for me to deliver Midian into their hands. In order that Israel may not boast against me that her own strength has saved her . . ." (Judges 7:2).

Is it possible to have too many men, too much time, or too much money? I would think more personnel, more time to plan and execute a project, and more resources would be good things.

But apparently that is not the case. God said that too much of anything leads to pride and takes away from the glory that belongs to Him. Sometimes I fail to move forward in obedience to the Lord because not having much makes me think I don't have enough. But God is more concerned that I trust Him to fulfill His promise than He is that I figure out a way on my own to make it happen. Without faith—without trust—it is impossible to please Him.

JUNE 6

As for me, far be it from me that I should sin against the LORD by failing to pray for you (1 Samuel 12:23).

The KJV uses the word *"ceasing"* rather than *"failing,"* which is the first way I learned this verse. I checked *Strong's Hebrew Dictionary* and learned the word *ceasing* comes from the primitive root meaning "to be flabby." OUCH! I end up sinning against the Lord when I am flabby, slack and sagging in the discipline of prayer. When I cease to pray for you, I am indicating how spiritually out of shape I really am.

God takes my spiritual condition seriously. Do I? I will check up on my prayer life again today. I don't want to sin against the Lord, nor do I want to fail you. God moves in response to my prayer because prayer changes me first and then others.

JUNE 7

But King David mourned for his son every day (2 Samuel 13:37).

Few things strike a parent's heart as deeply as watching one's child suffer physically, endure painful relationships, or die. A loving parent would gladly take his or her child's pain if possible. Even when suffering is a consequence of bad decisions, a parent grieves and bleeds right along with the wayward.

People of power, position, or privilege do not suffer any less than the rest of us. We all bleed the same color blood. Our hearts break, and our minds fill with if-onlys and what-ifs. And the pain continues long after the newspapers are thrown away, the TV reporters go home, and the neighbors forget. Was there anyone around to comfort David? A daughter had been violated, one son was dead, and soon another son would hang in the forest, his body pierced by multiple spears. We often sorrow alone—even in a crowd.

JUNE 8

The king of Israel answered, "Tell him: 'One who puts on his armor should not boast like one who takes it off'" (1 Kings 20:11).

Some people are big blowhards. They strut and brag, reminding you how important they are. Self-confidence is one thing, but they are ridiculous. If there ever was a great idea, it was *their* idea. If anything great ever was accomplished, *they* did it. If anyone was ever commended for anything, *they* were—and they can—and will—recite all the wonderful things others have said about them. These people would write their own flowery introduction. But there is a big difference between facts and flowers.

Elsewhere, Scripture says, "Don't brag about yourself—let others praise you" (Proverbs 27:2 CEV). There's a lot of "fighting" to be done between the time I put on my armor and when I take it off. I want to encourage others, not turn them off.

JUNE 9

My soul is weary with sorrow; strengthen me according to
your word (Psalm 119:28).

Sorrow will wear me out. It's only a matter of time. I may not be able to
change the details of what has happened. Irretrievable words have been
spoken; acts that inflicted their own special pain have been committed. I
may have been hurt beyond my ability to express it. Others have experienced
the same kind of conflict, disappointment, or bereavement, but this is my
pain, my grief, my sorrow. And I'm tired; tired of the memories, tired of
the tears, tired of trying to act like nothing's wrong. I'm weary physically,
mentally, emotionally—yes, even spiritually. I'm tired to the very core of
my being.

What can I do? I can cry out to the Lord and ask Him to give me
fresh strength to go on. I've found His Word has brought healing, faith,
comfort, and strength when nothing else could. Thank you, Lord.

JUNE 10

Speak and act as those who are going to be judged by the law
that gives freedom (James 2:12).

The word *law* brings to my mind rules, regulations, restrictions, the Ten
Commandments, stop signs, and a long list of other things that say I can't
do as I please. So how can they give freedom? Well, if I know and keep
them, my choice will prevent chaos, confusion, injury, and even death.

I need to play by the rules. I need to accept the limits set by the
regulations. Guiding principles help my life move forward more smoothly.
God gave the Ten Commandments, so they must be important to Him.
If my mind, emotions, body, or spirit are held prisoner in any way, it
may be because I have not spoken or acted according to the law that
gives freedom. True freedom comes with living life God's way. When I'm
pleased to do His will, I am free to do as I please. Ah, sweet freedom!

JUNE 11

Now Elisha was suffering from the illness from which he
died (2 Kings 13:14).

Some Christians are not compassionate toward fellow believers who get
sick and die. "They must have had sin in their lives," they say. "I wonder
what it could have been?" Or, "They didn't have enough faith," or give
enough, sing loud enough, or jump high enough.

Elisha enjoyed a double portion of Elijah's anointing, yet he got sick,
suffered, and died. He was not taken to heaven in a whirlwind as was
Elijah. Nor was he martyred as was Stephen and thousands of others in
the church.

Some feel that unless there is a miracle or at least a healing, there is sin
or unbelief present. Who says? Elisha and many others who have pleased
the Lord have gotten sick, suffered, and died. I'm just glad that for God's
people, sickness does not *end* in death (John 11:4a).

JUNE 12

My son Solomon, the one whom God has chosen, is young
and inexperienced. The task is great, because this palatial
structure is not for man but for the LORD God (1 Chronicles
29:1).

God chooses those who are young and inexperienced, which are not
detriments as far as He is concerned. Availability to the Lord, the condition
of the heart, desire, and obedience—those are the things that matter to
Him.

Yes, the task is great; we're talking about a work for a great God. We
must not downsize the vision to fit the age or experience of those God
has chosen. Remember, what God wants to build through us is not about
us. It's about Him. He chooses and calls the young and inexperienced
because, most often, they are uninhibited in their worship, wild in their
dreams, and daring in their faith. They do not know what won't work,
can't be done, is too big, or impossible. God will help and bless them!

JUNE 13

Some sat in darkness and the deepest gloom, prisoners
suffering in iron chains (Psalm 107:10).

Standing alone, torn from its context, this statement accurately describes
the experience of those who suffer from depression. They sit in what Saint
John of the Cross in the sixteenth century called "the dark night of the
soul."

Those familiar with depression through personal experience can tell
of the terrible darkness and deep gloom that follows and overtakes them
with a suffocating heaviness that can immobilize them for hours and days
at a time. Like prisoners held by iron chains, they suffer, unable to free
themselves, and unless help comes in time, they are in danger of losing
all hope.

I'm glad Jesus is the light for the dark places of my life. He lifts the
gloom and restores hope when I feel I am being held prisoner, bound in
iron chains. My Savior has tasted my suffering, and He has set me free.

JUNE 14

[Jehoram] passed away, to no one's regret, and was buried
in the City of David, but not in the tombs of the kings (2
Chronicles 21:20).

This verse is so tragic. I know that one of the non-negotiable facts of
life is that everyone must die. The only exception is for those the Lord
takes out of this world without their having to experience death. Enoch
and Elijah are two Old Testament examples, and those who experience
the rapture, the ecstatic catching away (1 Thessalonians 4:13-18), are the
others. But to live one's life and to die without anyone caring, missing
you, or regretting your demise—that is pitiful!

Jehoram's name means "exalted by God," yet he died alone in disgrace
and misery. I want to live in such a way that should I die before the Lord's
return, people will be glad for me and miss me at the same time.

JUNE 15

Rise up; this matter is in your hands. We will support you,
so take courage and do it (Ezra 10:4).

It's a wonderful thing to have people who believe in you, support you,
and encourage you. They become the wind beneath your wings. They
are your cheering section. They step over the line and join you in your
commitment to serve the Lord. They urge you on in obeying the Lord.

I've had people like that in my life. I need to remember that when
they identified themselves with me, they were putting themselves at risk.
They were committing themselves to the long haul. Their support was
not in words only; it included their time, resources, abilities, prayers, and
love. Whether the final result was a success or not, we were in it together.
"Thank you, Lord, for the wonderful people You've given to help me!"

JUNE 16

Dear friends, do not be surprised at the painful trial you
are suffering, as though something strange were happening
to you. But rejoice that you participate in the sufferings
of Christ, so that you may be overjoyed when his glory is
revealed (1 Peter 4:12-13).

New challenges arise and old ones recur. I keep waiting for things to get
better, for things to get back to normal. I'm still waiting. I've come to the
conclusion that "this" is normal. So rather than sit on the bench, waiting
for the bus that has been discontinued, I need to move on, take the next
step, do the next thing. Even if the trial is painful, even if the suffering
continues. This isn't strange—this is life.

Could it be I am to experience some of the sufferings of Christ? Could
this be the prelude to a greater joy than I could have ever dreamed of? It's
all about knowing Christ, and it will all be worth it when His glory is
revealed!

JUNE 17

You made a name for yourself, which remains to this day
(Nehemiah 9:10).

Nehemiah spoke these words after recounting the miraculous signs and wonders God sent against Pharaoh and Egypt. I like that. *The Cambridge Advanced Learner's Dictionary* [Cambridge University Press] defines "to make a name for yourself" as to become famous or respected by a lot of people. Is that what God did? Egypt's residents couldn't just pretend nothing had happened. But did He make Himself famous? I like this definition of the word famous: "very well known, excellent and satisfying" [*Encarta Dictionary*: English (North America)].

When God makes a name for Himself, He gains respect and holy awe; His excellence is well known and satisfying to Him and all who love Him. "O Lord, do it again. Make a name for Yourself in my life, family, and community!"

JUNE 18

Listen carefully to my words; let this be the consolation you
give me (Job 21:2).

Sometimes I don't need another sermon, another song, another Bible study, or another prayer meeting. I don't need another reminder of what I should or could have done differently. I don't need another pep talk about keeping a positive attitude. I don't need another major event with crowds of people. Sometimes I just need one person who will "listen carefully to my words." Someone who will listen without correction or comment. Someone who will listen as I attempt to put my innermost feelings into words. I may just need someone who will let me vent my frustrations, failures, and fears.

Let that be the consolation, comfort, and support you give me. Am I prepared to give that gift to someone else? That may be the greatest gift one friend can give another!

JUNE 19

He who walks with the wise grows wise, but a companion of
fools suffers harm (Proverbs 13:20).

I am known by the company I keep. The apostle Paul says, "Bad company
corrupts good character" (1 Corinthians 15:33 NIV). Sooner or later, it
will become apparent who my closest friends are, for they will influence
my decisions and behavior. My association with respected, honorable
people will lead to solid decisions and healthy relationships.

I will carefully select people who are known for their depth and
stability and get to know them better. Some of them I will gather through
books, reading the time-tested wisdom they have passed on. I will savor
times of conversation with present companions, considering their counsel
and cherishing their friendship as the special gift it is. I will choose my
mentors carefully, for I shall become like them.

JUNE 20

You open your hand and satisfy the desires of every living
thing (Psalm 145:16).

I have often met difficult days (and people) with a clenched fist, my
emotions in knots, my thoughts less than loving. Interruptions have
proven to be irritating to the inner peace I sought to cultivate. My body
language spoke louder than my actual words, and my patience wore thin
much too soon.

What if God were like me? I wouldn't want that—neither would
anyone else. I don't want God to be like me, and He isn't. He is not the
God of the closed fist; He is the God of the open hand. He patiently
listens to me, cares for me, provides for and protects me. He does not
always give me what I want, but I can count on Him to supply what I
need. If I begin to desire what He says I need, the sooner my life will be
full and my desires satisfied. He is the God of the open hand!

JUNE 21

He will wipe every tear from their eyes. There will be no
more death or mourning or crying or pain, for the old order
of things has passed away (Revelation 21:4).

Do God's people cry in heaven? This verse suggests they do. Read the
account of the redeemed who will stand before the judgment seat of
Christ (2 Corinthians 5:10). Will we be without emotion when we
learn of rewards lost because of wrong motives or worthless deeds? Will
we remain emotionless when we witness the fate of the lost standing at
the great white throne (Revelation 20:11-15) and hearing their eternal
punishment? I can easily believe we will shed tears.

Tears are no longer mentioned after the coming of the new heaven
and the new earth, for God "will wipe every tear from their eyes." Tears are
not forever, nor are death, mourning, or pain. What a glorious hope!

JUNE 22

If a ruler's anger rises against you, do not leave your post;
calmness can lay great errors to rest (Ecclesiastes 10:4).

Something needs to be said for those who stay at their post no matter
what. Blessed are those who hold steady, despite the freeze of criticism or
the heat of anger. When pressure mounts and tempers flare, it would be
easy to say, "Okay, have it your way" and quit. But no, this may be a storm
that will pass to be replaced by sunshine and fragrant breezes. Even if the
reprimand is deserved, staying calm and respectful will go a long way in
restoring the good graces of the one in charge.

There are too many variables to single out one outburst and make it a
reason for quitting. I must not leave my post. There are those who count
on me to stay calm. "Give me Your special grace, Lord, when I feel like
shutting down."

JUNE 23

Yet the LORD longs to be gracious to you; he rises to show you compassion (Isaiah 30:18).

It's hard to imagine a holy God not washing His hands clean of me. I can be a real pain some days, yet He longs to be gracious to me. Gracious would have been enough, but His *longing* to be gracious underscores and magnifies His tenderness toward me. I may be scampering around, doing my own thing, and unaware of His feelings toward me. My relationship with Him is not close while I'm dead set on having my own way. How His heart must grieve. He knows it is only a matter of time before I will be down, crawling back, wounded and defeated. I could imagine Him ignoring me, hoping I'll just go away. But look: "He rises to show (me) compassion." He does not hold me at a distance; He is actively engaged in giving me the good I don't deserve.

JUNE 24

Are they ashamed of their loathsome conduct? No, they have no shame at all; they do not even know how to blush (Jeremiah 6:15).

People don't start out in this condition. Even though I was born with a sinful nature, conscience told me when I'd done something morally wrong. But my conscience can become "seared" (1 Timothy 4:2) and callous if not heeded, less sensitive than it was before. Unconfessed sin results in a moral searing of my conscience, with scars that build up over time. Then the things that used to make me blush no longer affect me.

Shameless sinning is the result of a conscience that has been ignored and violated so many times that no feeling remains. Ezra modeled a healthy response (Ezra 9:6). "Lord, don't let me lose my ability to blush. I want to stay morally and spiritually sensitive."

JUNE 25

When I looked at you and saw that you were old enough for love, I spread the corner of my garment over you and covered your nakedness. I gave you my solemn oath and entered into a covenant with you, declares the Sovereign LORD, and you became mine (Ezekiel 16:8).

Boaz's response to Ruth acknowledged her desperate state, widowed with no close relative to care for her (Ruth 3:1-14). It was a symbolic act of his protection and provision and spoke of his willingness to marry her and take all responsibility for her care and wellbeing.

Ezekiel's passage speaks of the love covenant between the Lord and Israel. Like an unwanted infant, she had been cast out, rejected, and left to die. But the Lord saw her plight and responded, not out of pity, but out of love. This is a beautiful picture of what God has done for me. Unloved, filthy, left to die, God had mercy upon me and said, "I will make you mine." What a wonderful love!

JUNE 26

Great peace have they who love your law, and nothing can make them stumble (Psalm 119:165).

I find myself drawn to the Bible each day. I love to get up early in the morning, brew my first cup of coffee, and then sit in a comfortable chair with the Bible open on my lap. I love the feel and smell of the leather binding, the sound of the crisp pages as I turn them. I love to allow my imagination to enter the text, hearing the voices and watching the action. I try to experience the emotions the people I'm reading about must have experienced. Best of all, I love the sense of God's presence as His Holy Spirit impresses my spirit with the eternal truth before me, and I allow myself to respond, audibly or silently. My time in God's Word becomes dialogue, and my relationship with Him becomes fellowship. My soul is calmed, my faith is strengthened, and my walk with God becomes more confident.

JUNE 27

With flattery he will corrupt those who have violated the covenant, but the people who know their God will firmly resist him (Daniel 11:32).

Flattery is dangerous because it builds upon things that inflate my ego. If my self-esteem is low, and I'm doing a lot of negative self-talk, I'm in a vulnerable position for flattery to do its insidious work. Even when I know I'm not as good as the flatterer suggests, I listen because it makes me feel good at the time.

Flattery is a deadly tool if it affects my decision-making, causing me to favor someone because they have stroked my emotions with empty words. My guard against flattery is to remember God's covenant with me. By knowing who I am in Christ, I can resist cheap flattery that will only corrupt my mind and soul. God's Word to my soul is not flattery. It is transforming truth.

JUNE 28

But as for me, I watch in hope for the LORD, I wait for God my Savior; my God will hear me (Micah 7:7).

People watch for different reasons. Some watch out of fear or dread, forever staring at the horizon for the storm cloud they are convinced will appear to cover, smother, and destroy. Others watch with a suspicious eye, certain that someone is out to get them. They dare not let down their guard, for something bad or evil is sure to overtake them.

Micah's expectation was that good things were sure to come; it was only a matter of time. He was convinced God would hear him and answer favorably. Consequently, he watched in hope. He was waiting for the One who would not let him down. Let others worry; he would continue to expect the best.

June 29

Listen, O high priest Joshua and your associates seated before you, who are men symbolic of things to come: I am going to bring my servant, the Branch (Zechariah 3:8).

"Men symbolic of things to come . . ." Other versions of the Bible describe them as men who were signs, a wonderment, a portent. In this case, the things to come were good. These men pointed ahead to the Promised One who would come to set things right and bring new life—the Branch, or Christ. John the Baptist was a sign or portent as he cried out, "Prepare the way for the Lord . . ." (Matthew 3:3).

What about today? What about me? Am I a sign of things to come? Do I point the way to Jesus? Am I a portent, a warning, to those who carelessly disregard the message of His soon return? Am I fulfilling my life's purpose to be a symbol or depiction of the change Christ makes when He comes into one's life?

June 30

Then Jesus said, "Did I not tell you that if you believed, you would see the glory of God?" (John 11:40).

Jesus was not talking about believing for a miracle. It was believing in Him that mattered (see vv. 23-25). Martha answered well. She couldn't say she believed for the miracle, but she did believe in Jesus: "I believe that you are the Christ, the Son of God, who was to come into the world" (v. 27).

I've struggled so many times in believing for the miracle I thought I needed. My prayers went unanswered, my expectations disappointed, and my emotions frustrated. Little by little, my faith was stripped of every supporting argument until I was left with nothing but Him. And that was enough!

When I have nothing else but Jesus, I still have all I need. Believing in Him, I will see the glory of God.

July 1

Praise the Lord, for he has shown me his unfailing love. He kept me safe when my city was under attack (Psalm 31:21 NLT).

There was a time when I felt as though my "city" was under attack. The very place I thought would provide safety, convenience, comfort, and provision was under threat of danger and devastation. It seemed as though my life was about to be overtaken by a malevolent being—or perhaps a host of such beings, and I feared I might not survive.

Then one day, I realized I had been shown the unfailing love of my Lord. I would never have chosen to go through that time of uncertainty, misunderstanding, and emotional trauma, but through it all, I experienced a dimension of my Lord's love for me I could not have known any other way. I had been kept safe though not spared the experience.

July 2

The LORD . . . delights in the well-being of his servant (Psalm 35:27).

The Lord is happy when I'm happy—but it is much more than I once understood it. He "delights" when I am well. The Lord experiences pleasure and satisfaction when I am healthy, when I am whole, as wholeness involves spirit, mind, and body. Only when these areas are healthy and balanced may it be said that I am living in a state of well-being in the eyes of God. He delights more in my "being" than in my "doing."

My sense of well-being is connected to my having the attitude of a servant. A true servant is fulfilled when he has brought pleasure and joy to the heart of the one served. "The LORD . . . delights in the well-being of his servant." He loves it when my "doing" comes out of my "being." I want to be a servant today.

JULY 3

I broke the bars of your yoke and enabled you to walk with
heads held high (Leviticus 26:13).

The burden I've experienced may be best described as a heavy yoke around
my neck, the iron bars representative of the feelings of failure and the
conclusion of guilt, whether self-imposed or assumed by others. Rather
than enabling me to pull my own weight in life, this yoke hindered me.
It became increasingly difficult to look anyone in the eye. I struggled
through life with head bowed, shamed and criticized.

And then, when it seemed I couldn't take another step, the Lord
intervened. He broke the bars, removed the yoke, and enabled me to
walk with head held high. "Thank you, Lord. Because of You, I can live
confidently, looking life in the eye, without shame or arrogance."

JULY 4

Moses and Aaron and his sons were to *camp* to the east of
the tabernacle, *toward the sunrise*, in front of the Tent of
Meeting . . . (Numbers 3:38, emphasis added).

Morning is my favorite time of day, so when the phrase "camp . . . toward
the sunrise" stood out to me one morning, I was stirred with a longing to
experience this every day of my life. To me, the Holy Spirit was conveying
much more than a location—He was encouraging a discipline that
produces a positive attitude and saying I need to keep looking toward the
new day.

Yesterday is but a shadow; tomorrow is not yet here. I need to
intentionally focus on the reality of God's promises. If I live toward the
sunrise, I will not miss the wonder and glory of each new day.

JULY 5

The kind of death by which Peter would glorify God (John 21:19).

We usually do not think of death as glorifying God. Instead, we equate it with losing—the defeat of faith or coming to the end of life without accomplishing what others or we expected. The exception would be the martyrs of the faith. They gave their lives instead of compromising or recanting their faith in Christ. The word *martyr* refers to the ultimate witness.

Until Christ returns, we must all face death at some point. How we die is incidental, but the way we die is essential. Even in death, we can glorify God. "Lord, let that be true of me."

JULY 6

Even during the plowing season and harvest you must rest (Exodus 34:21).

The two most active and important times of the year for agrarian people are springtime, when the ground is prepared and seeded, and fall, when the harvest is brought in to the granary and barns. One might be able to slack off a bit during other times, but never these. Yet the Lord commanded that even during the "plowing season and harvest" His people were to rest. They *must* rest.

I may try to justify my many days and long hours by saying I am working for the Lord, doing the work of His kingdom. But even that is no excuse for my not resting. I *must* rest if I am to be my best! God said so.

July 7

But this happened so that the work of God might be displayed in his life (John 9:3).

These words spoken by Jesus appear in the record of the man blind from birth. The plaguing question in the minds of His disciples was, "Who sinned, this man or his parents, that he was born blind?" (John 9:1) Jesus' answer raised my eyebrows. A man is born blind, lives thirty or more years in that darkened condition, all so that "the work of God might be displayed in his life"?

I have questions of my own: How many others have been born with a physical handicap for this same reason? When did they discover the truth? Did the truth make the years of darkness, pain, confusion, accusation, or misunderstanding worth it?

Life happens. Will I permit the work of God to be displayed in my life?

July 8

A generous man will prosper; he who refreshes others will himself be refreshed (Proverbs 11:25).

I call this passage, God's Boomerang Blessing. Generosity, whether in material, emotional, or spiritual ways, will come back to bless the giver. But the one who is the recipient is not necessarily the one who returns the blessing. I am not to give to others with the thought that they will give back to me. Yet the fact remains and is confirmed by the Lord Jesus Himself, "Give, and it will be given to you. A good measure, pressed down, shaken together, and running over, will be poured into your lap. For with the measure you use, it will be measured to you" (Luke 6:38).

Do I need to be refreshed today? The answer is to reach out to refresh someone else. Then, at just the right time, God's Boomerang Blessing will return.

JULY 9

You fasten my feet in shackles; you keep close watch on
all my paths by putting marks on the soles of my feet (Job
13:27).

Job's statement makes me chuckle yet with discomfort. The mental picture
I have is of a meter maid marking the tire of a parked vehicle and then
checking back to see if it is still parked in the same place. That's the way
Job felt about God. If Job were in violation (had sinned), God would
surely know because He had put a mark on him that would reveal whether
he had gotten out of line or was just sitting still.

I leave a trail, good or bad, seen by God wherever I go. Sometimes my
violation is that I haven't done anything at all.

JULY 10

But I will rescue you on that day, declares the LORD; you will
not be handed over to those you fear (Jeremiah 39:17).

I may fear being "handed over." That could happen if I feel I've been
abandoned by those I had trusted, if the source of my confidence let me
down, had been unable to protect me, or worse, did not care enough to
stand by me to the bitter end. I might not only find myself alone, I might
find myself in the grip of the very ones I feared. What a terrible thought!

I love this verse because the Lord promises a rescue; He will not leave
me to the mercy of my enemy nor abandon me to the diabolical pleasure
of those seeking to destroy me. Whether real or imagined, those I fear are
denied access to my spirit. The Lord is my redeemer and rescuer.

JULY 11

The hand of God was on the people to give them unity of
mind . . . (2 Chronicles 30:12).

Unity doesn't just happen. It requires desire, hard work, and willingness
to compromise (but not morally) until the goal is achieved. Unity is the
harmony that makes progress possible.

Godly unity is the result of good people coming together, paying the
price, and refusing to settle for anything less. But even then there are times
when we just can't seem to get it all together. We meet, discuss, pencil in,
and then erase—investing hours of time and energy to no real end.

I like this message of hope: When the hand of God rests upon a people,
they can experience the reality of unity in their thinking, motivation, and
final outcome. Our Lord's desire is that we become one even as He and
His Father are one. "Lord, help me to do my part."

JULY 12

When the Lord saw her, his heart went out to her and he
said, "Don't cry" (Luke 7:13).

A dead son, a bereaved mother, a large crowd—and Jesus. The players
are all in place. But this is not drama, this is life, a setting typical of the
experiences we face in our own lives. Some things weigh so heavily upon
us they bring tears as our hearts spill over with pain. Family and friends
may offer sympathy, but there is little more they can do. We may even
wonder if Jesus cares.

Look at today's verse again. It's not that Jesus saw the woman or even
the words He spoke; it's the phrase, "his heart went out to her," that
touches my heart. That's compassion, love in action. It's what happens
when the love of Christ moves us and enables us to minister to others.
"Move my heart, Lord, with the compassion that moves yours."

JULY 13

And they praised God because of me (Galatians 1:24).

People are prompted to praise God when their lives have been redeemed by the blood of Christ and changed by the power of God. The evidence of His mercy and grace within us is a positive influence; our very presence reminds others of the faithfulness of God and causes them to rejoice with us.

Do people praise God because of me? Are they drawn to the Lord when they see me? Do they desire more of the Holy Spirit as a result of what they sense when I pray, speak, or just live my life from day to day? Do they thank God for me, or are they repulsed or disappointed by what they see?

JULY 14

And there was evening, and there was morning—the first day (Genesis 1:5).

The biblical day began in the evening and was already half over by the time the sun rose the next morning. In my view, the evening hours are the time to prepare for bed after a long day of work. But the biblical model suggests I need a good night of rest *before* I begin the tasks that await me. I am to start the day unconscious for most of the first twelve hours and accomplish nothing, as it is time to rest.

But God is at work, for He neither slumbers nor sleeps. In that sense, He goes before I enter into the new workday, and I wake up to continue the work He has already begun. The long, dark hours of the night, when I feel alone and unproductive, are filled with the proactive working of His Holy Spirit.

He prepares the day before me. I will wake refreshed and ready. It will be a good day!

July 15

You have instructed many . . . you have strengthened feeble hands. Your words have supported those who stumbled; you have strengthened faltering knees (Job 4:3-4).

The words of Eliphaz, one of Job's friends, were used as a setup for criticism. He did not intend for them to stand alone in a complimentary way. Yet in themselves they were factual, as they described Job's activity and its effect upon weak and needy people.

As I read these words, I wonder about the difference my life has made in the lives of others. Does my teaching enable others to gain confidence and hone their skills? Do my words encourage them in time of failure or defeat, enabling them to rise and walk with fresh courage and stamina? "Lord, let me be a blessing to someone today."

July 16

Moreover, Jacob deceived Laban (Genesis 31:20).

The name *Jacob* has been defined to mean, "heel grabber," "swindler," "cheat," or "supplanter," and today's verse reveals Jacob living up to his name. After his encounter with the Lord, however, his name was changed to Israel, meaning, "he struggles with God" (Genesis 32:28). Not only was Jacob's name changed, his life was changed.

Do I know what my name means? If not, I will look it up today. If the definition is complimentary, I will ask the Lord to help me live up to my name. If it is lacking in desirable qualities, I will remind myself that my spiritual name can be changed. Even if my given name is Jacob, by God's grace I can live in such a way that people will know I am one who has wrestled with God and secured the blessing! "Lord, may my desire for you result in a name that glorifies your name!"

JULY 17

In the morning, O Lord, you hear my voice; in the morning
I lay my requests before you and wait in expectation (Psalm
5:3).

I love the morning. It is my favorite time of the day. Everything is so fresh.
One may see the sunrise and find him- or herself filled with hope. One
may observe the dew on the grass or hear the song of a bird. The new day
arrives with the promise of better things.

David spoke of bringing his requests to the Lord, and the Lord hearing
him—in the morning. Having done that, he is able to wait in expectation.
The darkness of night is over. Problems may still exist, but they are better
dealt with in the light. It should be expectation, not foreboding, that
prompts my time with God. This is a great way to start the day. His answer
will be worth the wait!

JULY 18

"Why is this happening to me?" So she went to inquire of
the LORD (Genesis 25:22).

The most persistent, demanding question of all is "Why?" Small children
hound their parents with this question, and any attempt to give an answer
only succeeds in another, "Why?"

I know how important the whys are to me. All I'm seeking is a reason,
something to bring balance and sanity back into my life. The trouble is,
"why" questions usually go unanswered. They are not childish; they are
deep and profound, which is why pat answers or silence do not suffice.

Rebekah inquired of the Lord when she wondered about her unborn
babies jostling within her. In her case, she got an explanation. Might I get
more answers if I inquired of the Lord more often? Yet if He chooses to
remain silent, I will continue to love and trust Him—and wait.

JULY 19

Blessed is she who has believed that what the Lord has said
to her will be accomplished (Luke 1:45).

Blessed means "happy" but not in a shallow, happy-go-lucky sort of way. It is based upon an active faith that produces absolute certainty and contentment.

Mary's initial response to the angel Gabriel's announcement that she would be with child, the Son of God, was, "How will this be . . . ?" (Luke 1:34). Gabriel's answer satisfied her, and she embraced the promise. From then on, Mary experienced deep contentment.

I believe today's passage applies to everyone who takes God at His word. I am blessed, happy, and content in the God who will accomplish and fulfill all that He has promised. "Lord, help me to leave the details, procedures, and timing to You again today!"

JULY 20

Surely God is my help; the Lord is the one who sustains me
(Psalm 54:4).

The fact that God was his help says it all, yet David expanded on how God helped him. David was running for his life from godless, ruthless men whose single mission was to track him down and kill him. His self-talk was put to music because many could relate.

Sooner or later, everyone needs God's help. David reminded himself that God's help is not an "as needed" offer. It is a daily experience. David had come to know God as "the one who sustains me."

The Lord enables me to carry on and nourishes me so I can remain strong. I cease to be the victim when the Lord is with me, and I will remind myself of that each day. This is the healthy self-talk that strengthens my walk with God.

JULY 21

This is the day the LORD has made; let us rejoice and be glad in it (Psalm 118:24).

I've sung the praise chorus based on this verse many, many times and feel better even as I sing it. Certainly any day the Lord has made is going to be a good one! So I will respond to the invitation to "rejoice and be glad in it."

"Us" is a reminder that this is not a solo act, but more like a gathering, a party. So let's party! I like that. There is no danger that we could ever drain or deplete the blessing of the life God has provided us. Jesus said that He had come so that we may "have life, and have it to the full" (John 10:10).

God is pleased when I celebrate the new life I have in Christ. "Lord, help me to 'live the life out of' each day You give me!"

JULY 22

Friend, move up to a better place (Luke 14:10).

Wholesome friendship is enhanced by humility. There is a huge difference between confidence and cockiness, between being comfortable with who I am and flaunting myself in the pitiful effort to gain attention.

The parable out of which this statement comes was a lesson on humility. The man who took the lowly, obscure place at a prestigious event found himself approached by the host and told to "move up to a better place." Jesus expressed His heart; He desires to move us to a better place.

"For everyone who exalts himself will be humbled, and he who humbles himself will be exalted" (v. 11). The surest way to secure a "better place" is to avoid competing for it or presuming it is already mine. Humility is living life in right relationship with the Lord. If I do, in time His favor will promote me.

JULY 23

And treads on the waves of the sea (Job 9:8).

I find this expression by Job especially interesting. This man had such insight into the nature and activity of God and spoke of eternal realities, requiring a depth of spiritual understanding some yet struggle to find. For example, he spoke of seeing God in his flesh even after worms had destroyed his physical body, which is a marvelous glimpse into the new body we will one day receive at the Resurrection.

Here, Job describes God as the One who walks on water and "treads on the waves of the sea." Jesus, God Incarnate, did that, as recorded in Mark 6:49. Jesus not only commanded the stormy sea to be quiet, He walked its waves. He is the same God Job knew, and He's with me today, walking the stormy waves of my life.

JULY 24

I am still confident of this: I will see the goodness of the LORD in the land of the living (Psalm 27:13).

David had more than his share of troubles, as his heart for God made him a prime target for the attacks of the Evil One. Betrayed and forsaken by those he had trusted, fighting bouts of depression and suffering physical depravation, David was yet sustained by what he knew to be true, expressed in today's passage.

Where was that "land"? It was where he was at any given moment. David was a citizen of that land as long as he was able to draw his next breath. I must live my life with that same expectation and assurance today—and I can as long as my trust is in the Lord, the God who is good!

JULY 25

But Mary treasured up all these things and pondered them in her heart . . . But his mother treasured all these things in her heart (Luke 2:19, 51).

Twice it is written in Luke 2 that Mary treasured certain things in her heart, things related to her son, Jesus. We are not told that she ever shared those "treasured" things with anyone else. They remained guarded, valued, and precious; things she would think about when people criticized, ridiculed, rejected, and finally crucified her son; things that reminded her of the wondrous, miraculous, and divine moments that filled her memory as a result of who Jesus really was. Those things would hold her steady when the prophetic words of Simeon were fulfilled: "And a sword will pierce your own soul too" (2:34-35).

What things have I treasured in my heart?

JULY 26

Will I really have . . . now that . . . ? (Genesis 18:13).

Sarah struggled with God's promise of a son, which to her was ludicrous, preposterous, and absurd. Already way past childbearing years and married to a man ninety-nine years old, how much more ridiculous could it be?

We've all laughed at Sarah's thoughts and have agreed with her skepticism. The promise was beyond being too good to be true—it was crazy! But notice the way the Lord answered her, which is more telling than we care to admit and reminds me of the times I've scoffed at God's word: "Is anything too hard for the LORD?" (v. 14).

July 27

I have not stopped giving thanks for you, remembering you
in my prayers (Ephesians 1:16).

The apostle Paul set a wonderful example for us in being thankful for the
ones the Lord has put into our lives. Surely each of us could list the people
who have blessed us. But have we let them know we are thankful for them?
We've thought about doing it, but is that as far as it has gone?

Though I'm no better than most and worse than some, I have learned
that when I've made an intentional effort to put my thanks into words,
I've felt better, and I'm sure the recipient has been encouraged by it. When
it comes to prayer, I often work off a list, whether written or mental. Some
prayers are spontaneous as a name or face comes to mind. My desire is to
cultivate the spiritual discipline of regularly giving thanks and offering
prayers for those who mean so much to me.

July 28

On my bed I remember you; I think of you through the
watches of the night (Psalm 63:6).

Some people have trouble sleeping at night. They toss and turn, staring
into the darkness. They are not alone; four in ten adults sleep badly. Some
of this is related to sickness and disease. Other causes of sleeplessness are
worry, stress, life situations, and the like.

I've been blessed to be able to sleep soundly almost every night. Rarely
do I lay awake in the middle of the night, but when I do, I try to follow
the psalmist's example and make it a "holy insomnia" by using the time to
think about the Lord and pray for those I know are in need. Before long,
I'm back to sleep.

"My eyes stay open through the watches of the night, that I may
meditate on your promises" (Psalm 119:148). I can use my sleeplessness
to stay connected with the Lord.

July 29

At least there is hope for a tree . . . (Job 14:7-9).

I encourage you to read all three verses in this Scripture. The opening phrase caught my attention at a time when it seemed as though my "tree of life" had been cut down. While going through a difficult time of ministry, I read my Bible out of habit more than out of inspiration. And then, there it was: "At least there is hope for a tree . . ." As I read the words that followed, another phrase repeated in my spirit: *and there is hope for me.* Yeah, it rhymed, but more importantly, it reminded me of the God who promises to be with me. He is the one who can cause old stumps to spring forth with new life! I began to believe it could happen for my situation, and it did!

July 30

You hem me in—behind and before; you have laid your hand upon me (Psalm 139:5).

Sometimes I do not like the feeling of being hemmed in, as it suggests that I'm limited or controlled. But look at this verse again, and be blessed.

I see this verse as expressing how the Lord protects everything about me. He hems me in; I am not out of His care. "Behind" reminds me of my past; what happened then cannot be changed, but it is covered by His mercy. "Before" refers to my future, the details of which remain a mystery to me. Yet my future and all it holds is covered by His grace, which is sufficient. "You have laid your hand upon me" speaks of my present; I am covered today by His loving hand and feel His presence. I am not alone. I need not fear.

JULY 31

Because . . . because . . . (Genesis 22:16, 18).

When I was a young child, I drove my mother to distraction by asking "Why?" whenever she told me to do something. Depending on her level of patience, she may have tried to answer my query, but knowing how kids can be, I probably asked "Why?" again. "Because," she would say. "Because why?" "Because I said so, that's why" was the signal that I had run out of options. It was time to obey.

There is a direct connection between cause and effect. In today's verses, God told Abraham that because he had obeyed and not talked back, God was able to bless him in ways beyond his wildest dreams. "Lord, teach me to obey—just because!"

AUGUST 1

May he give you the desire of your heart and make all your plans succeed (Psalm 20:4).

"If I could just receive all that my heart desires, I would finally be happy." That's typical of the way many people reason in our day. Even we Christians are more eager to receive than we care to admit. But would we really be happy if God gave us everything we wanted? I doubt it would work for me. My own desires are much too fickle.

The secret is in having a heart embedded with desires that come from God. Psalm 20 was written by one described as "a man after God's own heart." I believe that what David is saying here and in Psalm 37:4 is that my delighting in the Lord results in His giving me the desires I need to embrace. And I can be assured that *those* desires He will satisfy. "Lord, give me the desires You want to fulfill in my life today."

AUGUST 2

"That is enough," the LORD said. "Do not speak to me anymore about this matter" (Deuteronomy 3:26).

There comes a time when all that can be said has been said. At that point, it does me no good to press the issue—even in prayer. No amount of arguing, pleading, threatening, begging, or interceding will change anything. Moses knew how to plead his case; he knew how to intercede for others; he knew how to camp on God's doorstep, refusing to budge. But God had already made up His mind, and the answer was no.

Is God's "no" the sign that all is lost? No. It simply means that my reasoning does not match His. God knows best—always. The apostle Paul prayed three times, earnestly, that his own situation be changed, but God answered, "No, but I'll give you the grace you need" (2 Corinthians 12:9). That was enough for Paul; it will be enough for me.

AUGUST 3

Now is your time of grief . . . In this world you will have trouble . . . (John 16:22, 33).

Well-meaning friends seek to affirm and comfort people, which they sometimes do by making statements that cannot be supported by biblical truth. The result is an unrealistic positivity that suggests difficulty can be avoided by emphasizing the positive. When that exists, people who struggle with perfectionism are devastated by less than positive experiences.

Should Christians expect a stress-free life? Not if we believe what Jesus says in today's passage. I need not be surprised by trouble, though I should not go looking for it. Jesus said it would come. I may even find myself bereft, filled with pain and sorrow. Perhaps this is my time of grief, but I must not stop there; I must not give up. Jesus said, "But I will see you again . . . take heart! I have overcome the world" (John 16:22, 33b).

AUGUST 4

The LORD made his people very fruitful; he made them too
numerous for their foes (Psalm 105:24).

Fruitfulness can be a matter of biological reproduction, so this verse could
refer to the increase of God's people, which resulted in their outnumbering
their enemies. But sheer physical numbers is not always the key to success
in times of conflict.

Fruitfulness is also a spiritual quality. Excelling and increasing in the
fruit of the Spirit, for example, develops in people who are strong and
mighty in the strength of the Lord. The working of the Holy Spirit within
each of us will produce a people who are too numerous (in spiritual verities)
for those who oppose us. We become "more than conquerors through him
who loved us" (Romans 8:37). I want to be in that number!

AUGUST 5

Jesus told . . . a parable to show them that they should always
pray and not give up (Luke 18:1).

Have you ever felt like giving up? Duh! Is the ocean wet? Is the sky up? Sure.
We've all had our times. Maybe that's why Jesus' parable has ministered to
me so many times. Just about the time I'm ready to throw in the towel, call
it quits, or give in to the frustration that comes with delay, I'll think of this
verse. Jesus devoted an entire parable to emphasize one simple instruction:
always pray, and never give up!

Praying brings me into harmony and acceptance with what God is
doing. So when I feel like giving up, Jesus says, "Don't. It's too soon to
quit! Keep on praying. Change is on the way."

AUGUST 6

Now the LORD was gracious to Sarah as he had said, and the
LORD did for Sarah what he had promised . . . at the very
time God had promised . . . (Genesis 21:1, 2).

The context is the birth of Isaac to the ultimate senior couple—Abraham
and Sarah. That noted, I will take a look at what these verses can mean to
me today.

The good that has been promised me will come because of God's
grace, His unmerited favor, which occurs apart from any of my efforts. My
part is to believe and trust—and often wait. But when it happens, it will
be what He promised and in His time.

I'm going to put my name into the text, which I refer to as "getting
into the Word." "Now the LORD was gracious to (_____) as he had said,
and the LORD did for (_____) what he had promised . . . at the very time
God had promised." I believe it!

AUGUST 7

But the more they were oppressed, the more they multiplied
and spread . . . (Exodus 1:12).

I love it! The Enemy of our souls must be thoroughly frustrated with the
people of God. And well he should be. His main objective has been to
totally annihilate anything and any one who could possibly bring glory to
Almighty God.

The Enemy is no lazy worker. He is focused, untiring, and powerful.
But the harder he and those with him work, the more the people of God
flourish. Do any of them experience setbacks? Yes. Do any of them suffer?
Yes. Do any of them die? Yes. Yet they are only temporarily slowed and
cannot be ultimately exterminated.

The same was true of the first Christians. Though hunted, persecuted,
imprisoned, and killed, the church continued to grow. Pursued across
the then-known world, the church has continued to live and preach and
triumph!

AUGUST 8

All the days ordained for me were written in your book before one of them came to be (Psalm 139:16).

Nothing takes God by surprise. Before I was born, before time began, God knew it all. So whether a person lives to see 969 years like Methuselah or dies in the early stages of human development, God knew it would be that way and had a plan as to how that life would have value and meaning.

As I read this message today, I rest in the certainty that God has a plan for me. My personal choices have not circumvented God's knowledge of who I am and where I am. Choosing His way assures me of life and blessing. Choosing my own way will result in consequences I do not want. My days have been "ordained," designed with my good in mind. I choose to go God's way today.

AUGUST 9

For today the LORD will appear to you (Leviticus 9:4).

One day during my daily Bible reading, the Holy Spirit quickened this statement to me, and my heart rate increased. It wasn't that I thought I would actually see the Lord in physical, tangible form; it was more an expectation that stirred within me.

As I ruminated on these words, I found myself going through my day with heightened anticipation that any moment might prove to be a "God Moment"—one filled with His divine presence. My heart longed that might be so. But there was preparation to be done; attention given to the condition of my heart. Would my words, behavior, motives, and attitudes be pleasing to Him? Would I even recognize Him?

What would your response be if you were told, "today the LORD will appear to you"? Would it be one of joy or apprehension?

AUGUST 10

Read Exodus 23:27-30

Little by little I will drive them out before you, until you have increased enough to take possession of the land (Exodus 23:30).

I found it interesting that when God brought His people into the Promised Land, He did not provide a quick and easy occupation. Though "promised" as far as God's people were concerned, the land's occupants were enemies. I would have thought wiping out the enemy immediately would have been the way to go. But no, it would not happen in a day—or even a year. God said, "Little by little I will drive them out before you . . ."

Of what use are the ungodly? Sometimes God uses them to help pay the taxes, provide merchandise, and enforce the laws of the land, although they are flawed. We are not always able to handle the administration of a new opportunity all at once. There are still too many "wild animals."

AUGUST 11

Read Psalm 91:14-16
Because he loves me (Psalm 91:14).

Many of us can quote bits and pieces from Psalm 91, as it is a favorite in times of difficulty or danger. I recall when I have drawn strength from this beautiful psalm. The statements are filled with promise, and I am comforted and encouraged. It closes with a direct quotation from God Himself. In short, pithy phrases, He offers a personal guarantee of deliverance, protection, answers to my prayers, His divine presence, commendation, longevity, and the revelation of His full salvation. *Wow!* (The line forms directly behind me, folks.) I want to cash in on this offer.

But wait. Go back, and read His reason for making such a statement: "Because he loves me." What level of love is God looking for? Elsewhere in Scripture, He says I am to love the Lord my God with all of my heart, soul, mind, and strength (Mark 12:30). Am I?

AUGUST 12

Jesus did not want anyone to know where they were, because
he was teaching his disciples (Mark 9:30-31).

Over the years, I've enjoyed attending silent prayer retreats, pastor-spouse
retreats, leadership retreats, etc. It's good to just get away from the "business
as usual" routine of one's life.

The absence of much of the distraction that clutters our waking hours
is soon apparent. Voices drop in volume. Steps are taken at a slower pace.
Light-hearted laughter accompanies the sheer pleasure of being with
people you love. Perhaps you sleep in a little later, or you take extra time
with the Lord. Conversations focus on things that matter deeply.

Jesus took His disciples aside to prepare them for the future. It was a
private time where He shared things not spoken to the masses. I want that
kind of time with Him!

AUGUST 13

Come with us and we will treat you well, for the LORD has
promised good things . . . (Numbers 10:29).

What a compelling invitation. There is no hint of selfishness or
manipulation. It's open and generous. Surely there will be an opportunity
for mutual sharing of talent and effort; that is only reasonable in a healthy
relationship. The invitation is warm: "Come with us." The status is
reassuring: "We will treat you well." And the prospect extends into the
future: "The LORD has promised good things." Whatever Moses was
offering was not limited by the present situation or supply. In effect, he
was saying, "We are willing to share the blessings God has promised us."

This is a good example of how I can be more engaging with people
today. I can invite, assure, and include them in the experience of receiving
that which God has promised. Let's make this journey together.

AUGUST 14

But as for me, I will always have hope; I will praise you more and more (Psalm 71:14).

I've identified *hope* as my favorite four-letter word. The common ones (ones you might expect) would be words like *love, life, work,* and *rest*—perhaps even *food*. But I'll stay with hope.

Someone coined the phrase, "Where there's life, there is hope." I've chosen to flip that statement to say, "Where there's hope, there is life." Hope grows out of the seedbed of trust, and trust is the expression of one's faith. The Old Testament in the KJV uses the word *faith* only twice, while the word *trust* is used over one hundred times.

My trust in the living God is what gives me hope, regardless of is happening around me. I will always have hope so long as I keep my trust in God. That's another reason to praise Him more and more!

AUGUST 15

Why do you just keep looking at each other? (Genesis 42:1).

I've been in meetings where the silence has settled over everyone like a heavy drape, and the very air is suffocating. Those in the room shuffle their feet, fidget with their pens, and roll their eyes. But nobody says anything; nobody does anything. Doesn't anyone have a valid idea that could lead to a possible answer? We just keep looking at each other.

Indecision *is* a decision. It is a decision to do nothing, to leave things as they are. We may not necessarily like where we are, but until somebody is willing to take the risk of pressing for a course of action that will change things, nothing will change. Someone must make the first move. Someone must lead. It's possible that decisions resulting in positive action will mean we "live and not die" (v. 2b).

AUGUST 16

Peace I leave with you; my peace I give you. I do not give to
you as the world gives. Do not let your hearts be troubled
and do not be afraid (John 14:27).

I do not offer this statement of Jesus today because I have some different
or special insight into it or because there was a day when it stood out in
glowing letters to me. I offer it because some days we need to be reminded
of the familiar.

You are no doubt one of the tens of thousands who can quote this
passage from memory. But just because you know it by heart is no reason
to skip over it with a casual, "I know that one already." Take some time
today to ruminate and enjoy again these very special words from our
Lord and Savior. Refresh your memory of the context in which they were
originally given. Consider where you're at today and the areas in which
you need His peace. Be encouraged and blessed.

AUGUST 17

Throughout the night, the cloud brought darkness to the
one side and light to the other side . . . (Exodus 14:20).

This was no ordinary cloud. It was the cloud of God's presence. Yet as
surely as one might expect that it would illuminate those whom it covered,
we are told it brought darkness to the lives of those who were enemies of
God and His people.

The Bible tells us that God is light and in Him there is no darkness
at all (1 John 1:5). So what is this all about? Here's a thought: You know
how dark, heavy clouds can make a day. Yet fly above the clouds, and
everything is bright and sunny. When God "stood" between His people
and the enemy, His glory was like a heavy cloud, with the "sunny side"
toward His people and the dark side toward the enemy. I call this the "dark
side" of God.

AUGUST 18

He will have no fear of bad news; his heart is steadfast, trusting in the LORD (Psalm 112:7).

Perhaps you've found yourself awaiting word following a battery of tests, X-rays, consultations, or exploratory surgery. Soon the waiting will be over, but the atmosphere hangs heavy with apprehension. What-ifs lurk like shrouded ghouls in the corners of your mind. What will the prognosis be? Should you be anxious? Certainly there is reason for concern or you wouldn't be here, right?

Many times as a pastor, I've shared this verse with brothers and sisters in Christ who found themselves in a situation such as this. How comforting it is to know that when we trust in the Lord we need not fear bad news. The key word is *fear.* There may be reason for concern but not anxiety. There may still be pain and adjustments ahead, but you are not alone. Keep trusting in the Lord.

AUGUST 19

Do not worry about what to say or how to say it (Matthew 10:19).

If you've ever faced accusations of wrongdoing, you know how anxious they can make you. Any advance time is spent going over the facts as you know them, anticipating the questions that may be asked and rehearsing how you will respond. The waiting often is worse than the meeting itself.

On the other hand, your answers may have significant influence on the outcome. Fines, imprisonment—even the sentence of death—may be based on your words. *What* you say and *how* you say it may make all the difference.

But worrying will not help. Jesus said the Holy Spirit is available to prompt us on what to say and how to say it. He will give you the words *at the time* you need them. I believe the Holy Spirit will help us even in our day-to-day personal and business dealings. Rest—but listen.

AUGUST 20

Because you did not trust in me enough to honor me as holy . . . (Numbers 20:12 NIV; see also Deuteronomy 32:51).

Moses was not permitted to lead Israel into the Promised Land. The most important reason was because Moses had not obeyed God's explicit command the second time God was going to provide water for His people out of the rock. The first time, God told Moses to strike the rock; the second time, Moses was to *speak* to the rock. But Moses *struck* the rock the second time. Both times, water came gushing out to slake the thirst of the multitude.

But God was not pleased the second time. Moses' disobedience had tampered with the prophetic picture of the coming Christ, sending the message that God was not holy enough to be obeyed. As a result, Moses suffered a terrible personal consequence. It is better to obey!

AUGUST 21

In the shelter of your presence you hide them . . . (Psalm 31:20).

Similar to Psalm 91:1, this verse draws attention to the *presence* of the Lord. It is a shelter for those who are in a time of trouble, a place of safety. We are hidden from the searching eyes of the Enemy. Evil is still active, but we are taken out of the action for a time. The battle between right and wrong continues, but we are given a personal respite. His *presence* is the shelter. His *presence* is the hiding place. To be present is to be here. His presence lets us know the Lord is with us. I like the words of the old hymn often sung by Ira D. Sankey in the D. L. Moody services: "In the secret of His presence how my soul delights to hide! Oh, how precious are the lessons, which I learn at Jesus' side! Earthly cares can never vex me, neither trials lay me low; for when Satan comes to tempt me, to the secret place I go; to the secret place I go." [*In the Secret of His Presence*, words by Ellen Lakshmi Goreh, music by George C. Stebbins]

AUGUST 22

I have prayed for you . . . (Luke 22:32).

Your Enemy desires to "sift you like wheat" (v. 31). You may not know when those times are about to come, but Jesus does. And He knows the severity of the action implied by those words. It's like being tossed into the air, exposing you to the blast of hot wind; in this case, the hot breath of the Destroyer. The Evil One's intent is to separate you from that which has served as the covering or protection for your life. He is not careful to "catch" you again, but hopes the shaking and tossing about will result in the loss of the wheat/life itself. Christ has forewarned us and then continues, "But I have prayed for you, (insert your own name here), that your faith may not fail . . ." (Luke 22:32).

"Pray for me, Jesus! Help me to endure, my faith stand strong. Amen."

AUGUST 23

You broaden the path beneath me, so that my ankles do not
turn (Psalm 18:36).

I've never been athletic and never really had an interest in being involved in sports. There's probably a reason somewhere, but I'm content as a spectator, enjoying physical prowess vicariously. Whether correctable or not, many times I've avoided joining in because of my weak ankles. A few good sprains along the way have taken the joy out of running and jumping. Even walking has proven to be risky. I don't need a hazard, though uneven ground contributes to the likelihood of an unexpected twist that sends me limping for awhile.

If you share my malady, you can appreciate my joy when I read these words of David. The Lord broadens the path beneath me so that my ankles do not turn. I can walk with the Lord today with the assurance that He is looking out for me.

AUGUST 24

For the LORD was merciful to them (Genesis 19:16).

My working definition delineating *mercy* and *grace* is this: *Mercy protects me from receiving the bad I deserve; grace provides me with the good I don't deserve.* In the context of Genesis 19 and 21, we find both words used, making their meanings very clear. In the case of Lot and his family in Genesis 19, we are told that the Lord was merciful to them in that He spared them the fiery catastrophe that came upon Sodom and Gomorrah. And Genesis 21:1 says, "The LORD was gracious to Sarah . . ." Sarah didn't "deserve" to have a baby in her old age nor was there anything she could do to cause herself to conceive. Yet, in God's time, she held her newborn son to her breast and laughed for joy at the goodness of God.

Grace and mercy are God's Siamese twins, inseparable. I need them both today. Don't you?

AUGUST 25

Oh, that their hearts would be inclined to fear me and keep
all my commands always, so that it might go well with them
and their children forever! (Deuteronomy 5:29)

I am struck by the intensity of God's words, which reveals His passionate desire. *Oh* is used to express the strongest emotion on God's part, and the exclamation point at the end of the sentence adds to the emphatic nature of what He said. This is the very heart of God, one of the things He is most passionate about: that His people would live in the fear of the Lord, keeping all of His commands *always*.

Does God need our obedience before He can be God? No. This is not about control. Fearing God, loving, honoring, and reverencing Him enough to obey Him, is the only way for life to go well with our children and us. And that's what God desires for us—*forever!*

AUGUST 26

I rejoice in your promise like one who finds great spoil
(Psalm 119:162).

Often we read and hear the promises of God with casual interest. We read
the Bible or listen to it proclaimed with a ho-hum attitude. Perhaps we are
bored; certainly we are lacking enthusiasm. After 161 verses about *the law
of the Lord, his commands, statutes, precepts, decrees*—all words the psalmist
uses to describe the Word of the Lord—he says, "I'm still excited about
what You have promised."

It has been said: "The future is as bright as the promises of God." Let
His promise bring you great joy today. Receive it with the excitement of
someone who has found rich treasure following victory in battle or who
has received the reward promised to a winner. God's promise says you are
victorious. His promise declares you the winner.

AUGUST 27

My intercessor is my friend as my eyes pour out tears to
God; on behalf of a man he pleads with God as a man pleads
for his friend (Job 16:20-21).

The most compelling, effective intercession is made by someone who
loves you, and no one loves you as much as a friend. Solomon declared,
"A friend loves at all times" (Proverbs 17:17). It is wonderful to have a
praying friend beside you as you cry out to God. He/she will plead with
God not just once or twice but repeatedly; as long as it takes.

Want to know who your real friends are? Take note of who prays *for*
you. Who kneels beside you, whose tears mingle with yours? Listen in, if
you have the opportunity. You will no longer feel alone in your struggle.
Your faith will be strengthened, your hope renewed. The Holy Spirit is
making intercession for you today, too—along with your greatest friend,
Jesus.

AUGUST 28

Make it your ambition to lead a quiet life, to mind your own business, and to work with your hands (1 Thessalonians 4:11-12).

Do you ever find yourself weary of all the noise? I do. I can't imagine how some people can even think when their lives are lived at high volume every waking hour. Yet I have experienced a few times when the very silence was deafening. Too much "head noise," I suppose.

Most of us don't list leading a quiet life among our higher aspirations. The apostle Paul, however, tells us that high-decibel living hinders us from having the best influence on those we want to win to the Lord. Quiet, unhurried, low-key living wins the respect of those whose lives are driven by stress and discord. Minding our own business while doing our best work leaves others watching us to want the stability and sense of peace we enjoy.

AUGUST 29

One thing God has spoken, two things have I heard: that you, O God, are strong, and that you, O Lord, are loving (Psalm 62:11-12).

The things I find most spiritual are those things that affect my life in the most practical ways. One day, I will live on the highest level (when I get to heaven), but for now, I need truth that works in my day-to-day relationship with God.

Of all the qualities of the Almighty, there are two I find most compelling: strong and loving. I need a God who is strong and powerful, able to protect and provide for me. He must be able to take care of the things of Earth and hell that threaten me. But I also need a God who is gentle and loving. I must feel that He is approachable and has my best interest at heart.

He is, and He does! I am safe and nurtured.

AUGUST 30

He did this only to teach warfare to the descendants of the Israelites who had not had previous battle experience (Judges 3:2).

This is the reason why the Lord left certain enemy nations to harass and threaten His people. Moses had died, and Joshua had died; we're talking about a third generation here. Things had settled into a predictable routine. It was manageable living but not victorious living, and the longer this continued, the greater the danger. So God allowed enemies to remain, whose only purpose was to provide a setting in which God could teach warfare to this new generation of chosen people. Would they obey the Lord's commands (v. 4)? Conflict would reveal that. God was not setting His people up for defeat, He was training them how to fight and win. Perhaps that's why we have battles to fight.

AUGUST 31

Then all the people shall say, "Amen!"
(Repeated twelves times in Deuteronomy 27:15-26).

"Amen! So be it!" was not a response to a question, such as, "Amen? Do you agree with me?" It was the response to a command: "Then all the people *shall say*, 'Amen!'" But notice what the people were commanded to say amen to. Six of the twelve tribes of Israel stood on one mountain to pronounce blessings on those who did what was right, and the other six tribes stood on the opposite mountain to pronounce God's curses on those who did what was wrong. Now, I can understand saying a hearty, "Amen!" to blessings. But God didn't tell them to say amen to the positive. He commanded them to say amen to what would come as a result of disobedience—curses—should they choose to practice things abhorrent in His eyes. Their "amen" confirmed their understanding and agreement. There are consequences. Amen!

SEPTEMBER 1

Those who know your name will trust in you, for you, LORD,
have never forsaken those who seek you (Psalm 9:10).

The TV quiz show *Who Do You Trust?* premiered in September 1957. An updated version of the question could be "Who *can* you trust?" as there is growing skepticism in a society where mistrust is becoming the order of the day. Barefaced lies are spoken with the same sincerity as "the gospel truth."

To trust is to believe with certainty, which enables us to surrender without fear of being betrayed, harmed, or taken advantage of. David made it clear that those who know the name of the Lord and His character will trust in Him. He is trustworthy in every area.

So, who do *you* trust?

SEPTEMBER 2

God has presented me with a precious gift (Genesis 30:20).

Not every woman feels this way. To some, the news she is pregnant comes with a chill down her spine, disgust, or worse. "This child is not wanted." "This pregnancy is an accident, a mistake. What an inconvenience." Or perhaps, "How will I explain this pregnancy to my spouse since it isn't his child?" "This isn't going to help my career plans." "There isn't enough income to support another child." "This isn't the right time. What's the best way to terminate the fetus?"

Jacob's wife Leah, however, didn't express any of these possible responses. She wanted the child enough to endure the normal inconvenience and discomfort of the pregnancy and welcomed the day of the baby's arrival. And when she saw him, she said, "God has presented me with a precious gift." What a wonderful welcome for the new arrival.

SEPTEMBER 3

But I am a man of prayer (Psalm 109:4).

God called David "a man after (my) own heart," (Acts 13:22) and here he refers to himself as "a man of prayer," but the two descriptions are inseparable. It's difficult to determine which flows out of which. Does prayer make us people after God's own heart, or is having a heart for God why we pray?

David did not describe himself as a man after God's own heart, but he does call himself a man of prayer. Speaking for myself, I want to be a man after God's own heart, but only God knows if and when that is so. It's a process that takes place as I yield to the working of His Holy Spirit in my life. My guess is that I have a long way to go. My next question is, Am I a man of prayer? Public observance is not what validates an affirmative response. But God knows. Both are a matter of the heart.

SEPTEMBER 4

All those who were in distress or in debt or discontented gathered around him, and he became their leader (1 Samuel 22:2).

This is not what you would consider a choice employment pool. If you were looking to build an army, create a company, or start a church, you would want people with the best education, talent, and personality. So give David a break. He was not recruiting people. He was running for his life. He was only interested in surviving and living to tell about it. But here they came—troubled, broken, hurting people in search of a leader. Difficult times were not over, but at least there was unity and cohesiveness that would bring fresh success. God gave David these people not just for his benefit but also for the good of all and the glory of His name. Who has God put in your life?

September 5

The men of Israel sampled their provisions but did not inquire of the LORD (Joshua 9:14).

How many times has our own reasoning resulted in our making a decision or arriving at a conclusion that we later learned was flawed? More times than can be detailed here. We could justify or explain ourselves by saying, "We did our homework. We studied the data. We included others in the process." That is commendable, a legitimate part of planning and decision-making, but it stops short of where we should have started.

We are not to form our decisions, make our plans, and then ask the Lord to bless them. The very self-assertiveness we think displays our maturity confirms our immaturity and lack of true spirituality. Genesis 1:1 records, "In the beginning God . . ." That's where this whole thing called life begins. Let's be sure we "inquire of the Lord" before we proceed. It will save us grief later.

September 6

The snare has been broken, and we have escaped (Psalm 124:7).

Have you ever felt trapped or imprisoned by a situation? Perhaps an addiction has dominated and controlled you for years. You've struggled, you've gotten counsel, you've asked friends for help, you've prayed. Yet nothing has changed. The struggle has left you weary, the counsel has left you confused, and friends have simply left you. Even God seems unaware and uncaring.

And then something wonderful happens: "The snare has been broken, and [I] have escaped!" You can't credit your own effort, the professional knowledge of a counselor, or the good will of your friends. What's left to be said? God has intervened. *He* has broken the snare. By His mercy and grace, you have escaped. You are free!

September 7

They may marry anyone they please . . . (Numbers 36:6).

I was raised to believe that there was a special someone for me, handpicked by God. My responsibility was to discover who that someone was. I did a little looking and placed an invisible question mark over the head of a few, a task that took years. I wasn't looking for the perfect specimen of femininity, but I was afraid of missing God's best for me. My future wife was designed in heaven especially for me, and I didn't want to settle for second best. The woman I eventually married has proven to be the greatest blessing in my life—second only to my relationship with Christ.

I would have had a difficult time saying our children could "marry anyone they please." Was this God talking? Yes. Read the whole chapter. You can feel good about this. Isn't God good?

September 8

Now write down for yourselves this song and teach it . . . and have them sing it . . . And when many disasters and difficulties come upon them, this song will testify against them, because it will not be forgotten by their descendants (Deuteronomy 31:19, 21).

Sometimes a song gets stuck in my head. I can't turn it off; it keeps playing, over and over. I find myself singing, humming, or just listening to it in my thoughts. Advertising jingles are designed to bring a product to your mind repeatedly, even when the radio or TV are not turned on. (I hate that.)

God instructed that songs filled with spiritual truth be written, taught, and sung, as they would serve as reminders of what He wants us to remember. I often "hear" them in the middle of the night or first thing in the morning. (I love that!)

SEPTEMBER 9

Go in peace, and may the God of Israel grant you what you
have asked of him (1 Samuel 1:17).

Hannah was barren, and for years she agonized over her desire to have a
child. Her husband could not console her. She wept and prayed, but even
the Lord didn't seem interested in helping her. She kept praying and drew
criticism from Eli the priest, who accused her of being drunk because he
couldn't make sense of her behavior. Yet Hannah's reply was respectful.
"Do not take your servant for a wicked woman; I have been praying here
out of my great anguish and grief" (v. 16). Then Eli spoke the words we
read in today's passage, bringing Hannah hope and assurance. "Then she
went her way . . . and her face was no longer downcast" (v. 18).

"Lord, help me not judge others by what I think. May I be sensitive
to Your Holy Spirit and speak words that will lift, encourage, and affirm
their faith in You."

SEPTEMBER 10

Have you suffered so much for nothing—if it really was for
nothing? (Galatians 3:4).

One day, while reviewing my struggles and sufferings (the makings of a
pity party, by the way), it seemed as though the Holy Spirit spoke the
words of this verse to me. I would not describe them as holy sarcasm, but
they sure got my attention. They silenced me and gave me something to
chew on. Soon I was out of my doldrums and back to glorious reality. (I'm
smiling now; I was sobered then.)

Could I really say all of my suffering was for nothing? Hadn't I learned
valuable lessons as a result? Had God abandoned me in my hour of need?
Was the sum total of my life a waste of time because it included painful
experiences I would rather have avoided? I got His message—and He got
my praise!

September 11

But I trust in your unfailing love (Psalm 13:5).

You can trust in the unfailing love of the Lord. God's love is the ultimate expression of unconditional. His love is without qualification, limit, or duration. He can't help Himself: "God is love" (1 John 4:8).

Be sure to remember, however, that it is impossible to love, in the truest sense of the word, without also hating. God hates as strongly and as unfailingly as He loves. His hatred is against any and all that threatens or contaminates those He loves.

You may have cut your teeth on John 3:16 while at your mother's knee. There is no contradiction in the Word. God's love flows to every person; His hatred is toward all sin and wickedness. God's love for you is certain, constant, and reliable. "Lord, help me to love what You love and hate what You hate."

September 12

He will keep you strong to the end (1 Corinthians 1:8).

I need this verse today. How about you? While I enjoy what I would consider good health, I still have my challenges. I don't feel sick, nor do I struggle with a debilitating physical handicap. But there are times—often—when I am reminded I am not strong, as in I am not physically powerful, brawny, or well-built. I never have been. As I age, I am aware of changes that slow me down and add areas of discomfort to my life.

But this is not my greatest concern. I need today's verse because I desire to remain *spiritually* strong and healthy. I want to stay in shape, regardless of what happens to me physically. There are plenty of reminders of where I still struggle in my walk with God. But here is the reassurance: "He will keep [me] strong to the end." That's what I want. I want to finish strong!

SEPTEMBER 13

Celebrating with all their might before the LORD (2 Samuel 6:5).

There is something so magnetic about a party atmosphere. Plans have been drawn, invitations sent, and preparations made. All is ready. Excitement builds as the day and time nears. And then . . . lights, sound, action. Guests arrive. Food and beverages are served. The music is turned up. There is laughter and loud conversation. Perhaps there is a dance. It's party time!

The ark of the covenant served as the reminder of the physical presence of the invisible God—the Lord Almighty. Its return from enemy hands was occasion to celebrate. And celebrate they did—with songs, harps, lyres, tambourines, sistrums, and cymbals. What a happy ruckus it must have been. I'm usually more subdued in my worship than that. But need I stay that way?

SEPTEMBER 14

Because the battle was God's (1 Chronicles 5:22).

If I'm trying to fight life's battles in my own strength, I should not be surprised with the outcome. No wonder I'm frustrated, exhausted, and defeated. The enemies I face outnumber my human resources and outpower my human reserves.

I should not expect the outcome to be different for me unless I follow the example of the Reubenites, the Gadites, and the half-tribe of Manasseh. Though numbering almost forty-five thousand men, they won the battle, not because of their numbers, but because they cried out to the Lord during the battle and trusted in Him (vv. 18-22). They defeated their enemies and plundered their goods. They still had to fight, but they won because the battle was God's.

When I trust in the Lord, my battle becomes His battle. And He never loses!

SEPTEMBER 15

From you comes the theme of my praise (Psalm 22:25).

An old (so old even Google® can't help me) gospel song contained the lyrics, "He is the lovely theme of my song," and today's passage may have been the inspiration for it. Too bad we're so into worship songs and choruses. Some of these, however, have lost touch with the theme, as the instrumentation and rhythm section have drowned Him out.

I have found myself caught up in the music rather than the Master. The wrappings have become a distraction, and I lose the wonder of His majesty and the glory of His name. I do not criticize the composers and musicians so much as I do my own failure to remember the heart of worship. I need to come back to the lovely theme of my song: Jesus.

SEPTEMBER 16

"I desire mercy, not sacrifice." For I have not come to call
the righteous, but sinners (Matthew 9:13).

Jesus drew hot criticism in His day for His modus operandi, and He draws criticism today through the behavior of some of His people who "eat with tax collectors and 'sinners'" (v. 11). I cannot justify "worldliness" by saying I must become like the world in order to win people to Christ. The end does *not* justify the means.

Jesus was not stretching the rules when He mingled with sinful people. He was living by *the* rule—the rule of heaven. He did not leave an example of compromise or of tolerance. He left an example of *mercy*. Jesus said He came to Earth to demonstrate His Father's love for wayward people, and He was right on task. Dare I follow His example?

SEPTEMBER 17

This is my name forever, the name by which I am to be remembered from generation to generation (Exodus 3:15).

I am one person, but I have many names. Some of them are titles or expressions of varied relationships. My children call me Dad. My grandchildren call me Papa or Grandpa. My wife calls me . . . well, none of your business (smile). My parents called me Son. Congregations called me Pastor. My friends call me Paul.

There is only one true God, but He has many names, each of which reveals something unique about Him. But of all His names, there is one that He said He is to be remembered by from generation to generation: I AM (v. 14). To me, this is so wonderful because it says He is God of the *now*, the God who is always and forever present. I need a God like that!

SEPTEMBER 18

If a person sins because he does not speak up . . . (Leviticus 5:1).

I've heard it said that silence is golden. Someone came along and added, "Sometimes it is just plain yellow."

We could avoid a host of interpersonal problems if we learned to keep our mouths shut. When tempted to say something inappropriate, untrue, or unkind, we had best bite our tongue rather than spew words that will offend or defame another human being. Sins of the tongue are especially damaging because, once spoken, they can never be taken back.

God, however, says that it is possible to sin by *not* speaking up. It is wrong to not confront or correct false charges brought against the innocent. It is wrong to let truth slide because we don't want to be inconvenienced by the commitment required to stand for what is right.

We will be held accountable for our silence.

SEPTEMBER 19

The LORD replied, "I have forgiven them, as you asked"
(Numbers 14:20).

I wonder if we really know and appreciate the power of intercession.
Moses interceded for Israel when the people rebelled against him as their
God-ordained leader. But their rebellion was much more serious than
that. God said, "How long will these people treat me with contempt? . . .
I will strike them down . . . and destroy them, but I will make you into
a nation greater and stronger than they" (vv. 11-12). Moses pleaded with
God to forgive their sin "in accordance with your great love" (v. 19). And
God did!

Jesus interceded from the cross, "Father, forgive them . . ." (Luke
23:34). And He did! As Stephen was being stoned, he cried out, "Lord, do
not hold this sin against them" (Acts 7:60). I must believe He answered
that prayer. Will we pray with the purity of heart that allows God to
forgive "as you asked"?

SEPTEMBER 20

For the LORD your God is a merciful God; he will not abandon
or destroy you or forget the covenant with your forefathers,
which he confirmed to them by oath (Deuteronomy 4:31).

The words *"he will not . . . forget the covenant"* stand out to me as an
irrevocable commitment on God's part, as they are a sacred pledge made
by the God who cannot lie. Are there contingencies? Yes. Are they in
the small print? No. God is forthright in stating the consequences of my
disobedience. But when there is a breakdown in my relationship with
God, it is not on His part.

Moses knew God as a covenant-keeping God. Despite the struggles of
my fallen humanity, He finds a way to keep His Word. He is a merciful
God. He will not abandon or destroy me as a result of forgetting His sacred
pledge, the covenant. My salvation is not based on my performance. It is
secured by His promise to all who believe. (See Titus 1:2.)

SEPTEMBER 21

Ignoring what they said, Jesus told the synagogue ruler, "Don't be afraid; just believe" (Mark 5:36).

I will not see the miraculous in my life if I listen to and take to heart everything others say. It's not that people are out to get me. Most who come alongside in my time of need are good, well-meaning people. I may have even followed their counsel on occasion. This time, however, they may not understand what God wants to do. To them, things have gone too far to change. Facts are facts. "'Your daughter is dead,' they said" (v. 35). Grieve, adjust, and go on. There are times when that is good counsel. But *this* time I may need to ignore what they said. This time, the Lord is saying, "Don't be afraid; just believe." I must pick out His voice from the crowd, and trust Him!

SEPTEMBER 22

Tell the people, "Get your supplies ready. Three days from now you will cross the Jordan . . . go in and take possession . . ." (Joshua 1:11).

Songs have been written associating the Jordan River with death, i.e., "I Won't Have to Cross Jordan Alone," which fit if the Promised Land is heaven. But I believe "crossing the Jordan" can represent crossing an obstruction into an area of opportunity and blessing here on Earth.

The Israelites were instructed to prepare for the crossing by getting their supplies together. "Three days" are significant, as that terminology is often used when speaking of death and resurrection. Some things have to "die" before we are ready to experience resurrection and new life. The promise is wonderful: "You will cross . . . go in and take possession." Get ready!

SEPTEMBER 23

Go! This is the day . . . Has not the LORD gone ahead of you?
(Judges 4:14).

When you have been praying about God's timing in your life, it is thrilling
to come across a statement like this in your daily reading of God's Word.
It may become a "rhema"—a living, spoken word to you. You've been
reading the "logos"—the written version—when suddenly it is as if the
Holy Spirit is speaking the words into your spirit. He now has your
undivided attention. It is not just part of the biblical historical record; it is
today, it is *now*, it is for *you*!

But be careful to not make every word a rhema word, for yourself
or anyone else, as that is the sovereign prerogative of the Holy Spirit.
But when He speaks, you will find a new level of faith and expectation
accompanying it and will be prompted to act on it.

Ask the Holy Spirit to speak to you every day, and you will discover
that He does.

SEPTEMBER 24

Her neighbors and relatives heard that the Lord had shown
her great mercy, and they shared her joy (Luke 1:58).

Burdens shared are divided, while blessings shared are multiplied.
Elizabeth's family and friends were aware of her years of struggle and pain.
She and her husband were highly respected, yet their godly living did not
guarantee them an easy life.

Elizabeth had hoped and prayed for children until there was neither
hope nor children. Now well along in years, she had resigned herself to
believing it was probably not to be, and her disgrace would remain to the
end of her days. But God had a different plan. (Read the entire chapter.)
The birth of her son filled her heart with song and her home with the love
and laughter of neighbors and relatives.

Find someone recently blessed by God and share his or her joy today.

SEPTEMBER 25

I prayed for this child, and the LORD has granted me what I
asked of him (1 Samuel 1:27).

There is nothing more persuasive than a praying mother. I had a praying
mother. She prayed for me before I was born and throughout my life until
her death. A mother may accomplish her most effective work when she
prays for her children. There is a lot to do besides pray, but a godly mother
considers prayer her first work when it comes to her family.

A mother knows how to pray *for*. Her prayers are the least selfish and
the most positive of all who pray. Hannah's testimony is this: "It pays to
pray for your children because God answers prayer. He answered mine by
granting me the desire of my heart to have a son who I could give to the
service of the Lord all the days of his life." Hannah's motive was pure, and
God was pleased to answer her prayer.

SEPTEMBER 26

How the mighty have fallen! (2 Samuel 1:19, 25, 27).

The national network news featured the announcement as its leadoff story,
accompanied by pictures of glory and shame. Sound bites added analysis
and commentary. The public sat in silence and then joined the verbal
reaction to what had been reported. First responses included disbelief,
shock, even jubilation. What was known was repeated, and the images
were shown over and over.

The person(s) involved were well recognized. They may have enjoyed
privilege and power, but now things had drastically changed. Wrongdoing
had been discovered, the details uncovered. Suspicion had been replaced
by charges, suspension, defrocking, prosecution, sentencing, and perhaps
eventual death. A career was terminated, a life ruined.

How do I respond to news of the fallen?

September 27

My prayer is not that you take them out of the world but
that you protect them from the evil one (John 17:15).

The hard cold evidence is that living in this world can be hazardous to our health and wellbeing. There is hardship, sickness, pain, and death. Knowing Jesus as Savior and Lord does not erase the facts of life for any of us, and God doesn't promise that life will be easy.

But Jesus did not pray that we should escape life; He interceded to the Father for our protection from the Evil One. Evil does not just happen; it is masterminded by the Evil One. Jesus prayed that those who have put their faith in Him would be protected from the one who directs the powers of darkness.

Will we continue to experience difficulty, hardship, sickness, and pain? Yes. But we need not fear the Evil One. The Father has answered His Son's prayer!

September 28

They were brave warriors, famous men, and heads of their
families. But . . . (1 Chronicles 5:24-25).

There are many good people in the world. Some of them are my neighbors. Others work in the gas stations, grocery stores, restaurants, clinics, and other businesses I frequent. They are pleasant, hardworking, and dependable. Some hold positions of power and responsibility. They are public servants committed to my protection and help in time of fire or accident. I see many of them enjoying their children and grandchildren. I see their pictures in the local paper with congratulations on reaching milestones in their marriages.

The people in today's verse may have been just like the people I see every day. "But . . ." That one word means I'm about to learn something that will change everything. "But they were unfaithful to . . . God . . ." Above all else, we must be true to the Lord!

September 29

He performs wonders that cannot be fathomed, miracles that cannot be counted (Job 9:10).

"Wonders" are the works of God that leave me speechless, a few of which I've experienced in my lifetime. Every time I remember them, I'm no further along in understanding them than I was when they occurred. "Miracles" are those events than can only be described as an act of God, as they contradict the laws of nature and scientific fact. Yet there is no denying their reality.

These words from today's passage are part of Job's description of the God he knows, the God who completes things I do not understand, the one who does the impossible without number, and calls those things which are not as though they were. Surely there is nothing in my life today that He cannot handle!

September 30

"Men, you are brothers; why do you want to hurt each other?" (Acts 7:26).

These are Moses' words from Exodus 2:13. I find this question more disturbing when put into the vernacular of the NIV. The antagonists fighting each other are brothers by national family, but their intention is worse. They *want* to hurt each other.

I was raised in an era when fellow Christians were referred to as "brother" and "sister." Moses' question brought me back to situations when I had witnessed conflict between believers. Though there was no physical injury, emotions and spirits were wounded. Things like this happen in families, and the deeper problem is most frightening. In the heat of battle, we often want to hurt the other person, set them straight, or make them feel our displeasure. We need to ask ourselves why.

OCTOBER 1

They will still bear fruit in old age; they will stay fresh and green (Psalm 92:15).

Age is a relative term, having little to do with the passing of time. When I was a child, I viewed people in their late twenties as old. Grandparents were *really* old. My own grandmother married at age sixteen. How old would she have been by the time her first grandchild was born? It's a scary thought. And "fossils" were in their seventies (I'm getting much too close.) You get the idea.

I need not fear outliving God's ability to use me for His glory. As I approach and then enter retirement, I am reassured that God has a place and work for me. But there is a qualifying description, however. Today's passage only applies to those who are among "the righteous" (v. 12), those who are living to please God. I want to be in that number. I want to stay fresh and green—and fruitful!

OCTOBER 2

That you and I may be mutually encouraged by each other's faith (Romans 1:12).

Mutuality is a wonderful word. It stands up and declares that no one needs to be alone in this thing called life, as there is an interconnectedness that is both essential and healthy. If I practice total dependence, I end up being a burden no one else wants to bear. If I insist upon total independence, I end up being alone. But interdependence . . . that is the kind of relationship I want to cultivate. As a Christian, I can say, "I need you, you need me, and we both need the Lord."

When we stand side by side, we are close enough to help each other. We can laugh, cry, work, celebrate, comfort, and cheer each other on. When I see you serving the Lord despite the difficulties in your life, I am encouraged by your courage and faith. I want to have that same effect upon you.

OCTOBER 3

On the mountain of the LORD it will be provided (Genesis 22:14).

A mountaintop experience sounds like the greatest of all experiences possible. Perhaps it is—for a mountain climber.

Peter, James, and John had a mountaintop experience the day Jesus was transfigured (Matthew 17:1-2). Abraham had a mountaintop experience when he offered his beloved son Isaac up to God, and at the last moment, God provided a lamb to take Isaac's place. This revealed what God would do for us when He offered His Son Jesus up for our sins.

We admire Abraham's faith and obedience. Notice the progression of the account: the test (vv. 1-2), the trek (vv. 3-8), the trust (vv. 8-10), and the triumph (vv. 11-13). Abraham is the father of all who believe (Romans 4:11, 16). He climbed his mountain knowing he could trust God. Am I up to climbing my mountain today?

OCTOBER 4

I would have poured out my heart to you and made my thoughts known to you (Proverbs 1:23).

Solomon personified Wisdom in the feminine mode. Wisdom's words in today's passage are especially warm and inviting. The context is the busy marketplace of our lives. There, we are surrounded by the influential voices of those lacking in moral direction; mockers and fools who hate knowledge. If heeded, they will turn our hearts away from God and His ways. So Wisdom "calls aloud in the street" (vv. 20-21), for what she has to offer is too good and too important for us to miss.

Wisdom expresses the very heart of our Lord. "Christ the power of God and the wisdom of God" (1 Corinthians 1:24). Christ speaks intimately to all who will listen, as He desires to pour out His heart to us. (Such beautiful words!)

Christ will share His thoughts with you. He desires an intimacy with you that will enrich your life. Will you listen?

OCTOBER 5

Who gave man his mouth? Who makes him deaf or mute? Who gives him sight or makes him blind? Is it not I, the LORD? (Exodus 4:11).

I was quick to number my "handicaps," as I was keenly aware of my limitations and flaws, some of which were in my personality. Others hid within my "skills" portfolio. I could think of more negatives about me than positives. Like so many others, I am not overly blessed with self-confidence and felt I could excuse myself by bringing out my "rubber crutches" whenever offered a new challenge. But rubber crutches will not support one's weight of responsibility.

And then I "heard" these words of the Lord in today's passage. He told me I was "flawed by design"—His design. He had made me with the abilities and flaws He was pleased to use for His glory, if only I will let Him. I'm still learning.

OCTOBER 6

To us who are being saved . . . (1 Corinthians 1:18).

I live among a vast number of people who are "being saved." They make great traveling companions. Their lives are promising, but not perfect. They are "in process," just as I am. None of us has "arrived," and we know it. Yet we are encouraged that it won't be much longer before we finish our journey and cross the final line.

I'm talking about the three stages of salvation. Past tense: I have been saved *by grace through faith* from the guilt and penalty of sin. Future tense: I shall one day be saved from the very presence of sin, never again to be tempted or threatened by sin. But now, present tense, I am *being saved*—saved from the power and dominion of sin. His "great salvation" (Hebrews 2:3) covers it all!

OCTOBER 7

I put . . . (Leviticus 14:34).

The Devil gets more blame than he deserves, and God doesn't get near the credit He deserves. We blame everything we deem negative on the work of the Evil One and assume everything positive has come from God. But when do we recognize the things that appear as "good" are actually being used against us by Satan and the things that appear as "bad" are used for our good by God?

"I put" in today's verse identifies the spreading mildew in the house as an act of God. He was teaching His people something they could not learn any other way. They needed to learn how to deal with bodies and lives that become contaminated by things that can prove deadly. "Thanks, Lord, for the things You put in my life."

OCTOBER 8

Aaron's staff . . . had not only sprouted but had budded, blossomed, and produced almonds (Numbers 17:8).

I believe God built age into His original creation, thus answering the question: Which came first—the chicken or the egg? The chicken did, a full-grown, mature hen. Nothing was created in an embryonic stage. But our first parents, Adam and Eve, were adults from the moment God made them.

Today's verse is an example of accelerated growth. Overnight, Aaron's dead walking stick "sprouted . . . budded, blossomed, and produced almonds." Typically, that just doesn't happen, as almonds require at least three years to produce.

Most things require time before they are complete, but God is able to bring things to pass before their time. Say it: "Whether by process or decree, God is at work in me."

OCTOBER 9

> For no matter how many promises God has made, they are "Yes" in Christ. And so through him, the "Amen" is spoken by us to the glory of God (2 Corinthians 1:20).

How many promises has God made to His people? Go through your Bible and count all you find. Another person may go through their Bible and come up with a different total, a few more, a few less. Let's not split hairs over the final count, as Paul said that is not what matters. The promises God made—*no matter how many*—are affirmed and confirmed in Christ. Every one! In His Son, the promises of God are stamped, "Approved." All that remains is for each of us to say, "Amen. Let it be so in my life."

When the promises of God for His people are received and activated in our lives, He is glorified. He made them, I act on them in faith, and Christ says, "Yes!"

OCTOBER 10

> To humble and to test you so that in the end it might go well with you (Deuteronomy 8:16).

God is not obligated to tell me why He does what He does or why things happen in my life the way they do. Yet His Word tells me enough to live with the peace of God in my heart, even when things are in disarray within and around me. Here is an example.

Moses reminded Israel of their journey through "the vast and dreadful desert, that thirsty and waterless land, with its venomous snakes and scorpions" (v. 15). God gave His people water out of the rock and manna from the sky. Their basic needs were met, but not much more. Why? To humble and to test them. "Well, thanks a lot! We have been humbled and tested beyond measure." Then God gave them further insight: so that in the end it might go well with them.

The purposes of God are for my good and His glory. I can trust Him.

OCTOBER 11

Consecrate yourselves, for tomorrow the LORD will do amazing things among you (Joshua 3:5).

I may not realize how close I am to seeing God do amazing things. It could be tomorrow! I may assume things aren't going to change that quickly, and my personal experience may attest to that. I've prayed and believed before, without any noticeable difference. So it has become harder to believe and easier to disregard. "Amazing things" sounds more and more like the hype from an overzealous preacher to whom everything and everyone is "incredible."

But preparation is required on my part before I can fully participate in what God is doing. This is called "consecrating myself" and is a holy activity. I must set myself apart for God and God alone. I must prepare my heart, mind, and spirit today if I'm to be ready for tomorrow!

OCTOBER 12

Power . . . (Ephesians 3:16, 18, 20).

I often notice how phrases in the Bible are connected through related words. This is true of the apostle Paul's writings.

In his letter to the Christians in Ephesus, Paul referred to power, using three distinct, fascinating phrases. The first is "with power." Paul's prayer is they might be strengthened in their very spirit by the Holy Spirit so that the life of Christ will be lived out in them. The second is to "have power" along with all the saints . . . to know and be filled to the top with the fullness of God. And the third is, "according to . . . power"—*His* power working in us makes all things possible.

October 13

Just after they had changed the guard (Judges 7:21).

The sweeping events found in the Bible are enhanced by the details we often miss in the bigger picture. The story of Gideon and the conquest against the oppressive Midianites is a case in point. Take three hundred unarmed men against the fighting machine of Midian? Unthinkable! Yet that's what God told Gideon to do.

The details of the record are there for more than adding to the suspense of the story. Notice this one. I would have thought it best to strike toward the end of one of the watches of the night, when the enemy was sleeping or so tired they were in danger of sleeping. But no, God chose "just after they had changed the guard." The ones going off duty were still awake and the ones on duty were well rested and alert. No problem. The enemy didn't have a chance. God said so. Victory was won.

October 14

The LORD . . . revealed himself . . . through his word (1 Samuel 3:21).

The Bible records several ways the Lord reveals Himself. It would make a wonderful study for you sometime. This one comes out of God's relationship with the young boy Samuel. The human-interest features of the account are worth reading for their own sake, as the innocence, respect, and hunger for God in this story would make any believing parent proud.

God had great plans for Samuel, plans that required him to know God in a special way. He would be a prophet of the Lord; God would speak to kings and nations through him. So Samuel would need to get the message straight and would need to know his source. God chose to reveal Himself to Samuel through his word.

Expect the Lord to use your time in the Word each day to reveal Himself to you.

OCTOBER 15

Being confident of this, that he who began a good work in you will carry it on to completion until the day of Christ Jesus (Philippians 1:6).

Paul thanked God every time he remembered the Christians in Philippi. His prayers were filled with joy because he knew these people stood with him in the proclamation of the gospel "from the first day until now" (v. 5). How could he be so sure these people would stay true to the Lord and loyal to him? By his assurance that the work the Lord had started in their lives would be completed.

Now let's apply that to our own lives. Are we confident, are we sure, that the One who loves us, saved us, and began to change us will continue that work until He has completed it? Fanny Crosby wrote, "Blessed assurance, Jesus is mine. O what a foretaste of glory divine . . ." [*Blessed Assurance*, Fanny Crosby, 1873] What Christ starts, He finishes!

OCTOBER 16

Because of his irreverent act . . . (2 Samuel 6:7).

The crowd numbering several thousand was in a party mode. It was loud—and wild. There was singing, laughing, and shouts of joy accompanied by a variety of musical instruments. Inhibitions had been set aside. It was an emotionally charged celebration of the highest order, and King David led the way. The people were ecstatic as together they "celebrated with all their might before the LORD" (v. 5). Our response to the Lord of glory must look dead in comparison!

But things got out of hand in the very midst of worship. Uzzah meant no harm when he reached out to steady the cart carrying the Ark of the Covenant, but suddenly he dropped dead in his tracks. God said he had committed an irreverent act.

Sincerity is not a substitute for obedience or exuberance for reverence.

OCTOBER 17

Ask for whatever you want me to give you . . . Moreover,
I will give you what you have not asked for (1 Kings 3:5,
13).

If I were in Solomon's shoes, what would I ask for if God came to me
and said, "If you could have anything you ever wanted, what would it be?
Name it, and I'll give it to you." Talk about an open-ended offer. I would
want to give my answer some thought. This would be the chance of a
lifetime! Did the Lord really mean it, or did I fail to hear the qualifying
statements? How long of a list can I have? What are the limits? Once
convinced the offer was valid, I'd want to give it more thought.

But Solomon's list was short, with only one request: wisdom to do
God's will. God was pleased to grant his request—and more. Is God as
pleased with my requests?

OCTOBER 18

I labor, struggling with all his energy . . . I am struggling for
you . . . (Colossians 1:29; 2:1).

In one verse, the apostle Paul says he is struggling *with* something, and in
the next verse, he is struggling *for* something. The word *struggle* speaks of
the effort spent in competing for a prize or contending with an adversary.
In this context, the prize would be the spiritual growth of the church and
the adversary would be the Devil.

In Paul's words, I see what is necessary on my part for those I love
and care about to do well: I must know, serve, and grow in the Lord, and
I must contend *with* the energy or power that comes from Christ. My
struggle must have a specific target. Paul said it was "*for you*" and those
beyond his immediate group.

I cannot avoid the struggle, but I can have the Lord's energy and
strength to empower me. I struggle for you, knowing the prize is worth
it!

OCTOBER 19

Then all the people left, each for his own home, and David returned home to bless his family (1 Chronicles 16:43).

To ignore the message in today's passage is to put those I love at risk. Being busy is no excuse for neglect. Does my schedule reflect only that I'm "important"—in demand to supervise, coach, help, lecture, manage, lead, administrate, or make the decisions to approve or censure? Must I always be the first to show and the last to go? I understand I have a responsibility to work and to work well. I am accountable. I must not shirk. But am I more important or busier than King David?

After worshipping the Lord and blessing the people (v. 2), King David's ministry continued when he returned home. I must make sure I do not forget to bless my family. I bless them with my prayers, my presence, and my passion.

OCTOBER 20

But my mouth would encourage you; comfort from my lips would bring you relief (Job 16:5).

I can relate to Job's questions, frustrations, and struggles. I concede that my situation is not as bad as his, and for that I am glad. But I can understand how someone would feel as he did and am amazed at how balanced he was in the midst of his dark night of the soul. Flashes of faith lit up his dark monologue as lightning brightens the darkest storm.

And then there are statements like today's passage. Rather than a feeble attempt to justify himself, Job's words reflect the warp and woof of his character. Acknowledging there were things he could have said to friends who were not "getting it," Job spoke as he normally would. Can the same be said of me?

OCTOBER 21

Therefore encourage one another and build each other up,
just as in fact you are doing (1 Thessalonians 5:11).

Encouragement is a necessary component of exhortation. Without it, our words come across as a reprimand, although gentle in their expression. The you-shoulds and you-oughts can come across as sterile or offensive. We may need to say them, but how much better if they are perceived as building up rather than correcting.

Encouragement comes out of the stands as a rousing cheer. Sometimes we need that too. The apostle Paul exhorted believers of his day to "encourage one another and build each other up" by adding an affirmation of his own: "just as in fact you are doing," which was like saying, "I like what you're doing. Keep it up!"

OCTOBER 22

The LORD confides in those who fear him; he makes his
covenant known to them (Psalm 25:14).

In today's verse, David refers to an experience most readily shared between friends. Remember when as a child you whispered into the ear of a friend and shared a secret with him or her? It was something you would not shout across the playground for all to hear. If quizzed as to why you were whispering, you might have replied with the bluntness of childish immaturity, "It's none of your business."

Our Lord has something to share that does not apply to everyone. It is for a select group: "those who fear him." Respecting the holiness of God enough to obey Him is the "fear" that qualifies us. Can you see Him motioning for you to draw nearer to Him? Can you picture Him bending to whisper in your ear? Can you imagine the wonderful things He would say to you?

OCTOBER 23

She is a tree of life to those who embrace her (Proverbs 3:18).

Solomon personifies Wisdom in the feminine gender. She cries out to the young and naïve. She gives counsel to those lacking in understanding. She seeks to turn the wayward from their foolish ways. She is valued above rubies. Nothing compares with her. She offers long life with one hand; riches and honor with the other. She is a pleasant companion to those who will follow her. And here, we are told, "she is a tree of life to those who embrace her."

"Lord, I want to be a holy 'tree-hugger.' I will embrace Wisdom and seek to follow in Your way—the way of life."

OCTOBER 24

As a dream comes when there are many cares (Ecclesiasted 5:3).

Do all of my dreams have meaning and significance? I hope not. Some of my dreams have no rhyme or reason that I can see. Others of them seem profound—until I wake up and consider the foolishness I've just experienced in my sleep. Some dreams are quite frightening, and I am relieved when I find myself safe in my own bed, the danger past.

Solomon offers one possible explanation for why we dream what we dream: "when there are many cares." Sometimes we can't shut our minds off at the end of the day. Too many situations concern us, and we carry our troubles with us into the subconscious state of sleep. Once in awhile, we wake up to discover that the answer came to us in the form of a dream, as God sometimes speaks to us that way (Joel 2:28; Acts 2:17). But dreams are a poor substitute for reality.

OCTOBER 25

Gave us eternal encouragement . . . (2 Thessalonians 2:16-17).

Some people will encourage you only so long as they still believe there is hope. When you miss the hurdle, don't reach the goal, or come up short in performance again and again, they become discouraged and lose interest in you. Where would we be if the Lord were like that?

Paul says that the encouragement that comes from above is "eternal encouragement." It transcends time and is not affected by our lack of natural ability or perseverance.

We give up when we no longer believe there is reason to hope. But God's grace working in our lives gives us "eternal encouragement and good hope." By that, our hearts are encouraged and strengthened in every good deed and word (v. 17). I'm glad the Lord hasn't given up on me!

OCTOBER 26

They parade their sin like Sodom (Isaiah 3:9).

Today's passage does not bless me, but it does strike me with its unerring, explicit description of the brazenness of sin. Each year, many communities celebrate "Gay Pride Day," with a parade and all. People of this lifestyle have long since come out of their closets. Tolerance has been replaced by acceptance. Some of us are still appalled by the cross-section of our society that is caught up in this behavior—young, old, wealthy, educated, those holding responsible jobs in high places, it makes no difference. But what we are witnessing today is nothing new. Isaiah saw it also.

The link to today: "They parade their sin like Sodom," a city known for its open homosexuality. Can we expect God's response to be any different? "Woe to them! They have brought disaster upon themselves" (Isaiah 3:9b).

OCTOBER 27

This is how you talk, but . . . (Jeremiah 3:4-5).

There are those who "talk the talk" but do not "walk the walk." They say all the right things. They feign a close relationship with God, but it is in word only. Even when their behavior is in open rebellion to the righteous ways of the Lord, they have the audacity to come back with, "My Father, my friend from my youth, will you always be angry? Will your wrath continue forever?" (vv. 4-5). Their attitude is presumptuous.

God, however, is not impressed with our talk—even if it's dressed in warmth and respect. He expects our talk to be confirmed by our walk. Jesus said, "Not all people who sound religious are really godly. They may refer to me as 'Lord,' but they still won't enter the Kingdom of Heaven. The decisive issue is whether they obey my Father in heaven" (Matthew 7:21 NLT).

OCTOBER 28

Yet this I call to mind and therefore I have hope: Because of the LORD's great love we are not consumed, for his compassions never fail. They are new every morning; great is your faithfulness (Lamentations 3:21-23).

I am blessed, encouraged, and strengthened whenever I read these verses. Living in the truth of the unfailing love and mercy of our Lord infuses me with the hope I need to face whatever comes my way. I am not dealing with a resource that may be depleted or exhausted at some point. If I were, I might wonder what I will do tomorrow, even if there is enough for today. I am not dependent upon the status of a "source"—my faith is in the Source of every good and perfect gift, whose love and mercy are "new every morning." I will make it today—and tomorrow, too!

OCTOBER 29

Cast your cares on the LORD and he will sustain you; he will never let the righteous fall (Psalm 55:22).

Life gets heavy. Just about the time I think I'm getting strong enough to handle it on my own—*WHAP!* I get broadsided and am stunned, staggered, and dropped me to my knees. (Well, at least I end up in the right position). The proverbial straw that breaks the camel's back pushes me over my limits. So why do I keep struggling on my own?

David said I am to cast my cares on the Lord. Not only will He help me because He cares for me (1 Peter 5:7), He will sustain me and hold me up. God's promise is that He will never let those who put their trust in Him fall beyond His reach or His ability to raise them up again. I will cast my cares on Him today!

OCTOBER 30

Christ Jesus came into the world to save sinners—of whom *I am* the worst (1 Timothy 1:15, emphasis added).

The apostle Paul's statement startles me. Perhaps it is a copyist's error or mere hyperbole. Perhaps it was false humility. Surely he was not the *worst* of sinners. Was he? Okay, so he was pretty bad when under the cloak of religious purity, he hunted down, imprisoned, and sentenced many of the first Christians to death. That was bad, but did that make him the *worst* of sinners? I don't think so. This was something deeper than a list of bad behavior.

And what of, "of whom I am the worst," in the present tense? Was Paul continuing a life of sin years after he had become a devoted follower of Jesus Christ? No, but daily he carried the knowledge that without Christ he *was* the worst. That's true godliness.

OCTOBER 31

I will . . . make the Valley of Achor a door of hope (Hosea 2:15).

My Bible defines "Achor" as meaning "trouble." Aha. I didn't realize it before, but I've been there. What a fitting description: the Valley of Trouble. The lyrics of an old American folk song just popped into my head, "Down in the valley, the valley so low; hang your head over, hear the wind blow."

My soul has felt the chilling blast when I've found myself in the midst of trouble. Boxed in by mountainous problems, I felt alone and frightened. Unseen enemies lurked in the deep shadows. I couldn't see my way out. And then the Holy Spirit brought a life-giving word to my spirit, and I discovered the very trouble I was experiencing had become a doorway of hope. The problems were still there, the accusing voices could still be heard, but there was a way out. I had hope. I had Jesus—the Way.

NOVEMBER 1

You . . . improvise on musical instruments (Amos 6:5).

Musical improvisation is to make up, perform, or compose on the spot without a set text to follow. Jazz is one of the great musical art forms known for improvisation. Other musical styles also allow for spontaneous, creative juices to flow between musician and music.

Now look at today's passage. Other versions speak of "inventing" the instruments themselves. Ruminating on the NIV wording, however, I pictured an Old Testament jazz ensemble playing songs written by David to glorify God. But they had gotten into ad-libbing, changing both music and words until the original message was lost. God was not impressed by their improvisation. Their spiritual complacency brought their feasting and lounging to an end (vv. 6-7). So much for all that jazz!

November 2

As you have done, it will be done to you; your deeds will
return upon your own head (Obadiah 1:15).

"Do to others as you would like them do to you."(Luke 6:31) The Golden
Rule remains powerful today. If I treat others the way I wish to be treated,
I will most likely receive kind words and loving actions in return. If I am
unkind in speech and behavior, I should not be surprised if I receive the
very things I have dished out to others.

God's Word through Obadiah declares the same is true for nations.
Am I praying for and contributing to the kind of life that will make the
nation in which I live more kind and loving?

November 3

But God's word is not chained (2 Timothy 2:9).

Nothing can change the character or power of God's Word. Unbelief
cannot destroy it, though my unbelief can keep me from enjoying its
blessings and benefits. Fighting it cannot hinder its effectiveness in the
lives of others. I may deny it, mock it, or fight it, but when the dust of my
fury settles, there it is, as strong, effective, and eternal as ever.

Outlawing God's Word from the classroom cannot keep it from
entering our schools in the hearts of believing students. Its truth stands
unchanging, its power never becomes impotent with age, and its light
never dims in the darkest night of sin. Others may gouge out my eyes to
keep me from reading it, cut out my tongue to keep me from speaking
it, chain my body to keep me from sharing it, but "God's word is not
chained"!

November 4

They have greatly oppressed me . . . but they have not gained
the victory over me (Psalm 129:2).

I once had an inflatable punching clown. It had a rounded, weighted
bottom that caused it to rebound to an upright position after being hit. It
was fun to box the clown, but it grew frustrating because it was impossible
to deliver a knockout punch. No matter how hard or how many times I
hit the clown, he always stood up again, smiling at me from behind his
big, red nose. I soon tired of the futile exertion and went on to other
things.

That childhood toy demonstrated the poise and position of the child
of God. We may be exploited, browbeaten, subjugated, and oppressed in
many ways. But, praise the Lord, we can testify, "they have not gained the
victory over me"! We say, "Thanks be to God who gives us the victory
through our Lord Jesus Christ" (1 Corinthians 15:57).

November 5

God provided (Jonah 1:17; 4:6-8).

If anyone is to be my provider, I want that someone to be the Lord! There
are no limits or shortages within the heavenly storehouse. There is not
only enough, there is *more* than enough. The riches of His abundance are
beyond my ability to comprehend or exhaust.

To say "God provided" is to say that He met whatever need in my life
with wisdom and generosity. The book of Jonah records four examples of
God's provision in specific detail. First, He provided a great fish (1:17);
second, He provided a vine (4:6); third, He provided a worm (4:7); and
fourth, He provided a scorching east wind (4:8). The fish and the vine
are examples of God's protection, and the worm and the hot wind are
examples of His discipline. I need both types of provision in my life.

November 6

Remember your journey (Micah 6:5).

All of life is a journey. For people of faith, it is a pilgrimage—a journey to a special, holy place. A journey spans the time and experiences between a starting point and a destination. The starting point is initiated by a decision, and the destination is the goal that promises to make the journey worthwhile. But it is the journey itself that makes all things possible. While the start is prompted by obedience and the destination is birthed by vision, the journey, or the process, is lived by faith.

I may not remember the actual date I set out, I may not know the actual date I will arrive, but it is extremely important that I "remember [my] journey." Journaling is the recordkeeping of my journey, referencing where I am today in relation to where I've been and where I hope to finally arrive.

November 7

Show me your ways, O LORD, teach me your paths (Psalm 25:4).

One's ways have to do with his or her behavior or habits, which describes who we are as the reason for what we do. We say, "That's just the way he is." Traditions are the details of one's way of life, the predictable things that make me recognizable to others. One's ways come out of one's character. In seeing the ways of the Lord, David would understand the nature of God more clearly.

Paths reveal the course or methodology of one's life, the trail left behind that others can follow. David desired to follow the Lord, to learn to live for God, so that others would not be lead astray when they followed him. I will make this my prayer today: "Show me your ways, O LORD, teach me your paths."

NOVEMBER 8

Your love has given me great joy and encouragement, because you . . . have refreshed the hearts of the saints (Philemon 1:7).

Paul was blessed as he witnessed others being refreshed and blessed by the love of his dear friend Philemon. His own heart was filled with joy and encouraged because of Philemon's life and ministry.

This verse tells me it is impossible to isolate my love so that it only touches one other person. Love seeks to refresh others at the deepest level, and if I have that kind of love, it will be impossible to prevent others from being affected by it. I may purposely intend to touch one life, but when it is Christ's love in me, other's are touched and blessed as well. I desire that others will be invigorated, energized, recharged, and filled with delight by what they see flowing out of me.

NOVEMBER 9

The LORD is good, a refuge in times of trouble. He cares for those who trust in him (Nahum 1:7).

The statement that God is good is an irreducible fact, an eternal given. Nothing can change that. To say He is a refuge in times of trouble tells me that He covers the myriad of troubles I may experience during a lifetime. Knowing the Lord is good and experiencing His protection—even when I'm not consciously aware of it—is dependent on my faith in Him.

Trust is the Old Testament word for *faith* and is used to describe the level of one's confidence and expectation in the Lord. I do not trust in His goodness—I trust in Him. I live in confidence that He loves and cares for me, that He has my best interests at heart, and that He will shelter and protect me in times of trouble. Trust is total dependence upon Him. It's not about how hard I try. It's about how much I trust.

NOVEMBER 10

LORD, I have heard of your fame; I stand in awe of your deeds, O LORD. Renew them in our day, in our time make them known; in wrath remember mercy (Habakkuk 3:2).

God is the Divine Celebrity. He has a reputation. His renown, though repeated in the conversations of the faithful, is not based on hearsay. If you've ever talked to someone who has been touched by His power or has experienced the miraculous done in His name, you will join those who stand in holy fear and wonderment, absolutely amazed. It will leave you wanting more. Not a "bigger and better" spiritual sideshow—more of Him!

To pray that He would "renew [His deeds] in our day" is to ask Him to continue making good on that which has established His fame and renown. And that is my prayer: "O Lord, make a name for Yourself in my life today!"

NOVEMBER 11

You lifted me out of the depths and did not let my enemies gloat over me (Psalm 30:1).

I had a friend in high school who, out of foolish fun one day, caught my wrist in the lid of a trash receptacle in the hallway. I couldn't pull loose. The harder I pulled, the harder he pushed on the swinging lid. My good-natured laughter turned to growing frustration. Then I became angry and wanted to hurt him back. He saw my mounting fury, wanted to turn me loose, but didn't dare, not knowing what I might do. The incident was resolved, but not before I had a painful mark across the underside of my wrist and had threatened him in a less-than-Christian way.

The Enemy of my soul taunts, teases, and threatens, trying to break me down. If he succeeds, he rejoices, struts, and may even leave me alone for awhile. But I need to run to the one who will "not let my enemies gloat over me."

NOVEMBER 12

(Made) the author of their salvation perfect through suffering (Hebrews 2:10).

Jesus was made "perfect through suffering." That thought messes with my theology, but in a good way. Why would the perfect One need to be made perfect, and through suffering?

I see "Jesus" as the name given to His humanity and "Christ" the name of His divinity. He never ceased being divine, and His humanity was sinless. Yet His humanity could be tempted and needed the same discipline as we do. Jesus' humanity was the servant, the instrument, of His deity, the part of Him that grew, developed, and became perfect, or mature.

Jesus' humanity learned obedience through what He suffered (Hebrews 5:8), so I can be perfected, or matured, through what I suffer. Jesus is my example; in following Him, God the Father is pleased.

NOVEMBER 13

Serve him shoulder to shoulder (Zephaniah 3:9).

A couple of pictures come to mind as I read today's passage. One is of a search party, looking for a lost child. Volunteers and professionals walk through the search area shoulder to shoulder, leaving no territory uncovered. The second picture is of an advancing army, moving forward shoulder to shoulder against the enemy, leaving no gaps between them.

To serve the Lord shoulder to shoulder suggests unity of purpose and concentration of effort, leaving no work uncompleted. The Lord is not looking for heroics as much as He looks for steadfastness. I will seek to partner with others of faith, whose only goal is to glorify God.

November 14

From this day on I will bless you (Haggai 2:19).

I felt I had come to the end of myself. I had prayed, repented, sought the Lord, begged, cried out, and believed—everything I knew to do—yet nothing had changed. Then one day while reading Scripture, this passage jumped off the page at me. Out of context? Yes, but the Holy Spirit used it to speak to my spirit.

Can you imagine how my perspective changed? Instead of feeling as though I was still in the dark, I found myself in the light. The Word had given an actual date—"this day"; the length of time—"from this day on"; and a promise—"I will bless you." I had a new spring in my step, and a new song in my heart. I don't recall what specific things I had cried out to God about, but the promise was enough.

I will walk in the assurance of His promise today!

November 15

He is like a tree planted by streams of water, which yields its fruit in season (Psalm 1:3).

Solomon said, "There is a time for everything, and a season for every activity under heaven" (Ecclesiastes 3:1). Fruit-bearing takes place "in season." Trees do not bear fruit the same time every year, as it depends on the kind of tree, its age, health, environment, pollination, and climate.

I believe there are parallels between the production of spiritual fruit in our lives (or the lack thereof) and natural fruit, as there are laws of the spirit and laws of nature. I like the statement of the apostle Paul: "In due season we shall reap, if we faint not" (Galatians 6:9).

NOVEMBER 16

Blessed is the man who perseveres under trial, because when he has stood the test, he will receive the crown of life that God has promised to those who love him (James 1:12).

"When he has stood the test" is the condition to receiving the promised "crown of life." This refers to a reward that follows salvation, not the acquiring of salvation itself. Salvation is ours "by grace, through faith . . . the gift of God" apart from works (Ephesians 2:8). Eternal life is part of the package that comes with salvation (John 3:16). Again, there's nothing here about our earning or deserving it. The crown of life, however, is something added or awarded to those who have "stood the test," stayed the course, endured to the very end.

Our involvement is required. Our standing the test has more to do with our trusting than it does with our trying. The crown of life is well worth the trial. Stand today!

NOVEMBER 17

Whoever touches you touches the apple of his eye (Zechariah 2:8).

"The apple of his eye" is an idiomatic reference to the iris, or center, of one's eye. If you get close enough to look directly into someone's eye, you will see your own reflection in that person's iris because the other person is looking directly into your eyes. Makes me think of what happens in a loving relationship. You become the apple of your beloved's eye and she or he is yours. So God said He would consider any enemy that touched you as poking Him in His eye. He would feel it, and it would be painful.

Our Lord has His eyes intently fixed upon those He loves. They fill His very vision. The Lord looks upon each us with love and cherishes us, as we are precious to Him. He takes it personally and is pained when His enemy hurts us.

November 18

Abraham was now old and well advanced in years, and the
LORD had blessed him in every way (Genesis 24:1).

I can understand Abraham being blessed by God, after all, he pleased
God as "the father of all who believe" (Romans 4:16 NTL). But notice to
what extent God blessed him: "in every way." Stop and consider what that
means. God blessed him in *every way*!

Way refers to categories rather than specifics, but that does not diminish
the power or scope of the word. I may never have a million dollars, the
body of a world-class athlete, or a mind like Einstein, and I may never be
the life of the party or walk on water. But I can be blessed *in every way*,
spiritually, mentally, physically, emotionally, and materially. I'll leave the
specific details up to the Lord.

November 19

I am still confident of this: I will see the goodness of the
LORD in the land of the living (Psalm 27:13).

I like the KJV of today's passage: "I had fainted unless I had believed . . ."
and the NLT: "Yet I am confident that I will see the LORD's goodness while
I am here in the land of the living." Any way you read it, David was both
realistic about his struggles and confident about the ultimate outcome.

Faith does not deny the fact of my struggle, but it operates with a
different set of facts—the promises of God. One fact says that my situation
is about to pull me under, but the greater fact is God is good, and I can
expect Him to come through in a way that is for my good and His glory.
Of that I can be absolutely confident!

November 20

These have come so that . . . (1 Peter 1:7).

I have asked, "Why?" when in the middle of difficult situations that challenged my mind, tested my stamina, and played havoc with the very things I thought I knew about God. Frustrated, I've wrestled with the issues, prayed the best I knew to pray, and sought any answer that would make sense.

God does not address my questions in any profound or explicit way. Usually it is not until I've worn myself out to the point of silence that His Holy Spirit speaks a word into my spirit that brings a peaceful sigh to my soul. Today's passage is one example: "These (trials) have come so that your faith . . . may be proved genuine and may result in praise, glory, and honor when Jesus Christ is revealed."

Thanks, Lord. I'm ready to face my day.

November 21

"And when they heard that the LORD was concerned about them and had seen their misery, they bowed down and worshipped" (Exodus 4:31).

It wasn't that the Lord was only aware of their misery; it was that He was *concerned* about them, meaning He was *interested* in them. With all due respect, that leaves me a bit cold, because I can be interested in something or someone out of curiosity. I may be intrigued by their story, but otherwise their situation doesn't affect me and requires no action on my part.

Another word is for concerned is *worried,* which speaks of anxiety that the Bible says is not to have a part in my life (Philippians 4:6). Besides, it's not very comforting to picture God as being worried about anything. But to think that He knows and is *concerned* about me . . . now, that's reason to bow down and worship Him!

November 22

As a gift to you (Numbers 18:6).

God gave Aaron a special gift: fellow Levites from among the Israelites. They were given "to do the work at the Tent of Meeting" (v.6). Christ gave apostles, prophets, evangelists, pastors, and teachers to His church "to prepare God's people for works of service" (Ephesians 4:11-12). In both cases, the "gift" was people.

I need to treat those God has put in my life as a gift. I will miss much of the joy if I am more taken up with their giftedness than I am with them as persons. I need to receive each person as a beautiful gift, wrapped in the ribbons of God's love. I may not say those exact words when I see or speak to them, but at the very least I want to say, "I thank God for you."

Expressing my love will raise my appreciation for them. I can only imagine how it will bless them!

November 23

From the lips of children and infants you have ordained praise (Psalm 8:2).

God intends for children and babies to praise Him. I must encourage them to do so. They will not praise the Lord the same way I do, but that doesn't make their expressions any less genuine or delightful to God. I needed to learn how to worship the Lord, and little ones can be taught also. I must be careful that I don't "dumb down" their experience to my expectations.

A child will be more uninhibited in praise if I stay out of the way, offering guidance and correction only as needed. As for infants, God recognizes and enjoys the purest praise that comes without instruction, only with permission. Intelligent praise may come with maturity, but remember, Jesus said, "Let the children come to me. Don't stop them! For the Kingdom of Heaven belongs to such as these" (Matthew 19:14 NLT).

November 24

A faith as precious as ours (2 Peter 1:1).

How high a value do I put on this matter of faith, either as a gift of God's grace, a spoken creed, or a life experience? My faith is precious because it is pure, personal, powerful, and priceless and has its source, focus, and fulfillment in God. He is the one who paid the highest price in order to ensure that my faith in Him would be effective.

Instilled by God, my faith is pure. Experienced in my life, it is personal. Released in my life, it is powerful. Valued by the people of God, it is priceless. I enjoy the highest level of fellowship with other human beings when I gather with those who have received and live by this same faith. We are people of "like precious faith" (2 Peter 1:1, NKJV).

November 25

But remember the LORD your God, for it is he who gives you the ability to produce wealth, and so confirms his covenant (Deuteronomy 8:18).

I just calculated my earnings over the past four decades. I had to estimate the average, of course, but I was shocked with the total. I am a very wealthy man! I didn't get all those riches at once; divided equally over those ministry years, my annual income was modest by most standards. But add in the benefits, perks, gifts, health, family, friends, opportunities of life, answers to prayer, and salvation. I never before realized the extent of God's blessing. The cumulative effect takes my breath away.

I am so blessed! God has been so good to me. What do I have that God hasn't given me? (1 Corinthians 4:7). And in that, He confirmed His covenant, His holy promise. Take a few minutes to count your blessings today.

NOVEMBER 26

One of you routs a thousand, because the LORD your God
fights for you, just as he promised (Joshua 23:10).

Much of the warfare in Joshua's day involved arrows, spears, and
hand-to-hand combat. There were no grenades, assault rifles, or bombs;
each individual was a fighting machine. As a result, casualties were high
on both sides. There were brave, courageous warriors then as there are
now, but even with the best, you would not put one man up against a
thousand.

Joshua said one of God's fighting men could put a thousand of the
enemy to flight because God Himself was involved, present to engage the
enemy on behalf of His people. It was His promise. I too can expect a
victorious outcome even when I feel outnumbered and overwhelmed. The
Lord my God will fight for me. I'll just show up (Exodus 14:13).

NOVEMBER 27

But as for me, it is good to be near God (Psalm 73:28).

Opinions are a dime a dozen. Everyone has one, even if he or she doesn't
have a dime, and I've heard it said that everybody is entitled to his or her
opinion. But opinions do not carry weight until they become convictions,
which must be personally held or one may only be following the crowd.

Joshua told the people of his day to choose the god they wished to
serve. "But as for me and my house, we will serve the LORD" (Joshua 24:15
KJV). Samuel said, "As for me, God forbid that I should sin against the
LORD in ceasing to pray for you" (1 Samuel 12:23 KJV). And David said,
"As for me, I walk in my integrity" (Psalm 26:11 RSV). I want to live by
my convictions, not by my opinion—or anyone else's.

NOVEMBER 28

The reason the Son of God appeared was to destroy the
devil's work (1 John 3:8).

To appear is to become visible. Something may have been present all the
time, but I am not aware of it until I see it. While I realize I have other
senses that support the reality of something I cannot see, today's verse uses
significant terminology.

We do not see the Devil in physical form, but we can surely see his
work. Pornography, illicit drugs, acts of violence, and loss of life and
material goods are indelibly etched into the record of human experience.
The evidence is dark, raw, and bleeding, and our ears pick up the moans
of despair, the shouts of anger, and the screams of fear and pain—things
we see, hear, and feel. But Jesus *appeared* in human form to destroy, in
real time, many of the visible results of the Devil's work. One day, He will
remove the Enemy himself!

NOVEMBER 29

March on, my soul; be strong! (Judges 5:21).

I like the self-talk statements in the Bible. This one from today's passage
comes from "The Song of Deborah," which was originally sung as a duet
between Deborah, a prophetess and judge in Israel, and Barak, a nervous
commander in the Israeli army. I wonder how their voices sounded
together.

At his commissioning, Barak told Deborah, "If you go with me, I
will go; but if you don't go with me, I won't go" (v.8). So Deborah went.
After a stunning victory over Sisera, commander of the Canaanite army,
Deborah and Barak sang their special song, which recounted the events
surrounding the battle. Halfway through the lyrics comes this powerful
statement: "March on, my soul; be strong!" This reminds me that I need
to take charge of myself today and speak words that keep me in the
battle—as long as it takes.

November 30

He will guard the feet of his saints (1 Samuel 2:9).

Surefootedness is critical to one's progress and ultimate well-being. To lose your footing on the edge of a precipice could mean a fall that leaves you with broken bones. To lose your balance could prove to be more than an embarrassment. Poor traction and control could cause you to lose a game where running and turning are key elements in making a touchdown. But to slip in the midst of battle could put you in mortal danger.

In today's passage, Hannah expresses her understanding of God's promise in the plural sense: "He will guard the *feet* of his saints." He will safeguard my steps on life's pathway. Because of Him, I can proceed at a sure and steady gait. Let me link this with the words of David: "If the LORD delights in a man's way, he makes his steps firm" (Psalm 37:23 NIV).

December 1

I will . . . fulfill . . . vows my lips promised and my mouth spoke when I was in trouble (Psalm 66:13-14).

There's nothing like trouble to keep me on my knees—the best place to be when I'm in trouble. Perhaps that's why trouble is good for me. I'm not looking for trials, but when they come, I'll admit I'm more willing to seek the Lord.

I say I want to stay closer to Him—and I do—but why does it take trouble before I put my desire into action? Human nature, I guess. Also, the problem often affects the level of my promises to Him.

Vows are sacred promises and are not to be casually spoken. God can hold me to my vows. I need to be sure that when I am in trouble I only make promises I will keep. I can't bargain with God and then renege. Are there any vows I have made to God while I was in trouble that I have failed to make good on? Today is the day to follow through!

December 2

And this is love: that we walk in obedience to his commands
(2 John 1:6).

Love may be expressed in words, but it is demonstrated by actions. In
today's verse, I am told the best way I let God know I love Him is by
obeying Him. In fact, this is the only way I can show Him that my love is
genuine, not just empty words.

The love expressed in words is the love expressed by the Lord in His
commands. Whether I hear them as comforting or correcting, they all
come out of His heart of love. Even the most confining of His commands
is based upon His love for me. Though they may restrict my pleasure,
they are not given to curtail my joy. So my response to the things God has
commanded should be obedience. When I obey Him, I show Him that I
love Him. How much of my love for God will I demonstrate today?

December 3

God does not take away life; instead, he devises ways so that
a banished person may not remain estranged from him (2
Samuel 14:14).

Not much is said about the one who made this statement in today's passage
except that she was "a wise woman" (v. 2), who had spoken these words to
King David after he and his son Absalom had become estranged. David
longed to see Absalom again but didn't know how to go about reconciling
with him. Should he, or should he not?

This sordid story provides me some understanding of David's dilemma,
as the wise woman's words remind me of the heart of God when people
have estranged themselves from Him. He "devises," or works out, ways so
the people don't have to remain separated from Him anymore. Do I work
for restoration in my relationships?

December 4

If today you will be a servant to these people and serve them and give them a favorable answer, they will always be your servants (1 Kings 12:7).

Leadership requires vision, focus, conviction, and confidence, both a gift to be expressed and a skill to be learned. The margin for error is extremely narrow when national security or human life is at stake. King Rehoboam, the son of Solomon, suddenly found himself in charge when his father died. What should he do? The public cry was for change: Go easier on us, and we will serve you.

Give Rehoboam credit for checking with the elders, who counseled him in today's passage to take the position of a servant, but call him to account for not heeding their advice. Heavy decisions are more readily accepted when mandated by those committed to serve. Be a servant leader, and people will gladly follow you.

December 5

You are the God who performs miracles; you display your power among the peoples (Psalm 77:14).

I need a miracle-working God, as there are needs in my life beyond my ability to satisfy them and areas of bondage I am unable to break. There are perplexing problems for which I have no solutions. Viruses and disease wait in the shadows along my pathway, waiting to assault me and deprive me of health and strength. Unseen enemies of the spirit world plot my spiritual demise.

I need a miracle-working God in more ways than I know. I will lift the eyes of my faith to the God who performs miracles, leave the "how" and the "when" to His flawless wisdom, and trust His unconditional love and mercy. I will then see His power displayed in my life and in the lives of those I love.

DECEMBER 6

We're not doing right. This is a day of good news and we are keeping it to ourselves (2 Kings 7:9).

Desperate people may become selfish in the name of self-preservation. Human nature kicks in and pushes them through whatever or whoever stands in their way. A break received is not necessarily a break shared. Who knows what future calamities lay ahead? It seems reasonable to store, to hoard. So grab all you can get, and hide it away from the eager eyes and reaching hands of others. It's every man for himself in this dog-eat-dog world. Why should I share information that allows others to receive the same benefits as I? There is enough for me but perhaps not for the two of us.

I am ashamed of those times I have withheld the good news from others. The gospel is meant to be shared.

DECEMBER 7

It was for the sake of the Name . . . (3 John 1:7).

I want my life to be governed by the highest motives. "Because" is the lowest of reasons I could give. "Just because" is no better, as it may only reveal my personal preference. I may be adrift rather than anchored. I may have my aim on that which is immediate or on that which I believe to be easily attained. My family and friends deserve better than that from me.

A godly professor from my college years often reminded his students that any dead fish can float downstream, but it takes a live one to swim against the current. The most worthy cause I embrace will energize me for the greatest effort for the longest period of time. John the Beloved wrote of those who "for the sake of the Name" did what they did, resulting in glory to God. I want that to be the motivational standard of my life today!

DECEMBER 8

Saul died because he was unfaithful to the LORD (1 Chronicles 10:13).

Everyone will die, the only exception being the faithful who are yet alive when Christ returns. So I will die if Jesus tarries in coming. The clock is ticking for each of us; good, bad, indifferent, wicked, godly—all of us will die (Hebrews 9:27). Some die of old age, others of accident, violence, or disease. But we all die. It is the constant reminder of the fatal consequence of Adam's sin. Innocents die, criminals die, infants die, centenarians die, and everyone in-between.

Saul's unfaithfulness to the Lord was the reason he died when he did. He would have died anyway, but what a tragic commentary on the reason for his demise. Even the troubled prophet Balaam knew the difference. He said, "Let me die the death of the righteous, and may my last end be like theirs!" (Numbers 23:10).

DECEMBER 9

He reached down from on high and took hold of me; he drew me out of deep waters (Psalm 18:16).

I remember the first time I jumped off the end of the swimming dock as a child and didn't touch bottom. I stretched my legs downward, expecting to feel the lake bottom beneath me. It didn't happen. I went all the way under and felt a wave of panic. I dog-paddled vigorously, turning back toward the dock where I clung to one of its legs until I had regained my composure.

I've often laughed when someone says I'm "deep." For me, that simply means I'm in over my head, and I've been "deep" more than once in my lifetime. How reassuring to know there is One who reaches down, takes hold of me, and draws me out of deep waters! When I'm in over my head, I call, and He's there to help.

DECEMBER 10

But as for you, be strong and do not give up, for your work
will be rewarded (2 Chronicles 15:7).

The Holy Spirit delivered a special message to King Asa through the prophet
Azariah that I believe is applicable to all who, like Asa, do right in the eyes
of the Lord. Surrounding nations were in turmoil and the people were far
from God, yet when Asa called out to the Lord, he received this life-giving
answer in today's passage in response to his faith and obedience.

I can't control the beliefs or behavior of others, nor can I mandate
their support or change their mind-set. I can seek to influence others in
the ways of the Lord, but I can't make them commit to active involvement.
I want to make a difference and be a blessing. The Holy Spirit says to
me, "But as for you, be strong and do not give up, for your work will be
rewarded." I will continue to press on.

DECEMBER 11

Called . . . loved . . . kept (Jude 1:1).

My heart is warmed just reading these words in today's passage, as they
describe my life in Christ. I am called "out of darkness into his wonderful
light" (1 Peter 2:9), I am loved "with an everlasting love" (Jeremiah 31:3),
and I am kept by the One "who is able to keep (me) from falling and to
present (me) before his glorious presence without fault and with great joy"
(Jude 1:24).

Back off, you who want me to believe there is no purpose for my
being, who say I am unloved, and whisper that it is only a matter of time
before my weakness will prevent me from finishing strong. Those are all
lies! I choose to believe the Word of the Lord that says I am called, loved,
and kept! In Him, I live and move and have my very being (Acts 17:28).

DECEMBER 12

Everyone whose heart God had moved . . . (Ezra 1:5).

Positive things happen when God moves upon the hearts of people. Hearts once closed are opened. Minds once resistant become supportive and creative. Fists once clenched, relax. Voices once filled with anger soften with expressions of love. Stingy grumps become generous givers. The complacent and indifferent become passionate and committed. Those set in their ways become set on *His* ways. Carelessness is replaced by carefulness. Unbelief is replaced by faith. Dry eyes and empty altars are filled with the tears of the penitent and the shouts of the forgiven.

Wonderful things happen when hearts are moved by God. Move mine again today!

DECEMBER 13

When I called, you answered me; you made me bold and stouthearted (Psalm 138:3).

A profitable study is to look up all the ways the Lord answers our prayers, what He supplies, and how He deals with us. His answers always target our deepest need rather than our whimsical wants. Did David ask God to make him bold and stouthearted? Maybe not in so many words, but in today's passage this is obviously what he needed most at that time. Being courageous and resolute carried into other areas of his life as well.

When I call out to the Lord, I will express my request as best I can, based upon what I believe I need. His answer—and He does answer—may come in a different form than I expect, but I can accept it as what I need at that point in my life, and it will be more than enough. God's answers are not limited to single issues. They minister to my entire being.

DECEMBER 14

Remember the height from which you have fallen! Repent
and do the things you did at first (Revelation 2:5).

Here's a three-point outline based on today's verse: 1. *Remember*—I
remember the way things used to be. I may remember a time when my
relationship with the Lord was intimate and growing. Perhaps it is only
a memory because it may not describe my relationship with Him at the
present time; 2. *Repent*—Repentance is a change of mind and direction.
I need to repent only if I'm going in the wrong direction or my thinking
has influenced my relationship with the Lord in a negative way. It's time to
make some changes; and 3. *Repeat*—This word is not in today's passage,
but the meaning is. If I remember a time when I enjoyed closeness with
the Lord but I'm not experiencing that now, the way to change that is to
do again what I did then. *Remember, repent, repeat.*

DECEMBER 15

We prayed to our God and posted a guard day and night to
meet this threat (Nehemiah 4:9).

As a child, I was taught to fold my hands, close my eyes, and then pray.
Folded hands kept me from playing with a toy during prayer time. But
there were times I was caught peeking, looking around while others were
praying, which was definitely a no-no. When I opened my eyes during
prayer, I was immediately distracted by what was going on around me.

At first, I prayed prompted and then memorized prayers. My first "solo
flights" were very childish, I'm sure. The instruction, however, helped me
learn the disciplines of prayer. When I first read Jesus' words, "Watch and
pray" (Matthew 26:41), I learned it was important to know how to pray
with my eyes open. In praying, I talk to God. In watching, I keep an eye
out for the Enemy.

So pray and watch. Post a guard.

DECEMBER 16

And these are but the outer fringe of his works; how faint
the whisper we hear of him! Who then can understand the
thunder of his power? (Job 26:14).

Job had a profound understanding of God, which resulted from his close
relationship with the Almighty. Without the help of a telescope, Job gazed
into the heavens and saw the handiwork of the Creator. The Holy Spirit
probed his inner man and stirred a consciousness of the holy. Job was
overwhelmed by what he saw and the thoughts that filled his mind. Yet,
he knew "these are but the outer fringe of his works; how faint the whisper
we hear of him!"

The greatness of God witnessed in our human condition is as a
whisper compared to the fullness of His glorious being. One day we will
experience the thunder of His power! Hallelujah!

DECEMBER 17

Till I entered the sanctuary of God; then I understood their
final destiny (Psalm 73:17).

Life isn't fair. It is filled with contradictions and conundrums. The horizontal
view does nothing to answer my questions or satisfy the disappointments
of life. Human perspective only leads to the further distortion of perceived
values. No wonder so many are frustrated. The inconsistencies of life
will affect me, too, unless I spend time in the presence of God, where
clarity is added to impression and balance is restored to my hopes and
expectations.

I must not judge the alleged success of the ungodly by the size of their
income, their opportunities, or their influence. Where they appear to be
is not the final word on where they are or where they will be. I like Asaph's
conclusion: "I entered the sanctuary of God; then I understood their final
destiny." I will look up. I live by faith, not by fate!

December 18

But Jesus often withdrew to lonely places and prayed (Luke 5:16).

Crowds of people came to hear Jesus and be healed of their many infirmities. He spoke with authority. His touch brought healing from chronic and terminal of conditions, and news about Him "spread all the more" (v. 15). It was the best kind of publicity, but Jesus was not looking for publicity; He was intent upon doing His Father's will.

Jesus often withdrew from the crowds and the excitement of the miracles He performed and found a lonely place where He could pray. Secluded, free of distractions and demands, Jesus prayed. This was not a worship service; this was a prayer meeting, time spent with His Father. A time to entreat, a time to listen. Jesus then returned with renewed power and clear vision. I need time like that today.

December 19

When you lie down, your sleep will be sweet (Proverbs 3:24).

There are few things worse than tossing and turning all night long. The day may have been difficult, things await my attention tomorrow, or I may be dealing with the discomfort of sickness or the pain of injury. What I need is a good night of rest. Staring at a dark ceiling, watching the numbers on the digital clock advance or listening to the cacophony of intruding thoughts is not my idea of a good night. Eternity for the lost may be something like a night that never ends.

Solomon spoke of lying down and enjoying a sleep that is sweet. That's more like it; that's what I'm looking for. Such rest comes from the Lord. Real rest, sweet dreams. Yes, Lord!

DECEMBER 20

You have given me hope. My comfort in my suffering is this:
Your promise preserves my life (Psalm 119:49-50).

Hope: my favorite four-letter word. It tops work, home, food, life, even love. Without hope, nothing else matters. The psalmist sang, "You have given me hope."

The Word of the Lord brings hope to the heavy heart. I may need to endure suffering, but I can take it; I can make it as long as I have the promise of the Lord, which is one reason I read His Word each day. I need the consistent, habitual intake of His good promise. My life is preserved because of it, my soul is comforted by it, and my spirit rises on strengthened wings as I meditate on it.

God's Word is His bond. "Be sure of this: I am with you always, even to the end of the age" (Matthew 28:20 NLT). I have Him; I have hope!

DECEMBER 21

Do not be overrighteous, neither be overwise . . . Do not
be overwicke . . . The man who fears God will avoid all
extremes (Ecclesiastes 7:16-18).

Extremes—life is filled with them. The reversing point of a pendulum marks its point of extreme travel, whether to the right or the left. In astronomy, apogee marks the point farthest from an orbited object; perigee, the point nearest. Each is an extreme.

Solomon wrote about avoiding extremes. He struggled in this area and knew the dangers, yet he fell victim to extremism more than once. It is not good to be either prodigal or overcautious. Some people are so heavenly minded they are no earthly good. Others are so worldy minded the kingdom of heaven is foreign to them. Balance is the result of centeredness. If my life is centered in Christ today, I will avoid extremes and fulfill God's good purpose for me.

DECEMBER 22

But will God really dwell on earth with men? The heavens, even the highest heavens, cannot contain you. How much less this temple I have built? (2 Chronicles 6:18).

Solomon did things on a grand scale. His mind envisioned magnificence, and he knew how to get things done. Neither finances nor manpower were ever a problem. The temple project was successful, and the building was stunning. Yet a nagging question was expressed the day the temple of the Lord was finally dedicated: "But will God really dwell on earth with men?" This question reduced the building to its true proportions.

Solomon's best efforts fell far short of accomplishing his highest hopes. What was he thinking, entertaining the possibility of God actually dwelling on Earth with humankind? I think God smiled, for He knew what *He* had in mind: One day, He would really dwell among us! (See John 1:14).

DECEMBER 23

Ask the LORD your God for a sign . . . the LORD himself will give you a sign: The virgin will be with child and will give birth to a son, and will call him Immanuel (Isaiah 7:11, 14).

King Ahaz was at a critical point in his reign in Judah. God told him to ask for a sign that would be the proof of His presence and help. But Ahaz refused, not wanting to be guilty of "putting the LORD to the test" (v. 12). But neither the prophet Isaiah nor God were pleased.

Acting on God's Word in faith is not presumptuous. Ahaz tried God's patience, but God did not give Ahaz what he deserved. That's mercy. "You won't ask me for a sign; I will give you a sign." The sign would be the birth of Immanuel, meaning "God with us."

Jesus was the flesh-and-blood proof that God cares! In Him, all of the promises of God are "yes, and so be it" (1 Corinthians 1:20). I have had my *righteous reluctance* overridden by the grace of God more than once.

DECEMBER 24

"I am the Lord's servant," Mary answered. "May it be to me as you have said" (Luke 1:38).

Mary's response to the angel Gabriel's unexpected visit in today's passage includes relationship, surrender, and faith. This life-changing announcement was that Mary would give birth to the Son of God. Relationship is where it began: "I am the Lord's servant." Surrender comes out of her servant's heart. And together, faith was activated.

My relationship with God determines the level of my surrender to His will. Do I live my life with the desire to serve Him? If so, I can surrender all that I am and have the pleasure of His will. I can trust Him. When that is true, He imparts faith that makes all things—even impossible things—possible. I will search my heart. Who knows? Perhaps His Word will come to me today. I want to be ready.

DECEMBER 25

Thanks be to God for his indescribable gift! (2 Corinthians 9:15).

How do you say thank you for something so wonderful it defies description, something so large you can't take it all in? Something so precious you fear losing it, so unique you know there could never be another one like it? Something so full of meaning you can't comprehend it, so simple you can't misunderstand it? Something so priceless you could never afford it, so abundant you could never exhaust it? How do you say thank you for something you've never seen yet love more than anything you've ever held in your arms? What words do you choose to express feelings that go beyond your ability to articulate them?

Say, "Thank you!"—but not to another human being. Let your thanks be to God for His indescribable gift: Jesus. "Thank God for his Son—a gift too wonderful for words!" (NLT).

December 26

And having been warned in a dream not to go back to Herod, they returned to their country by another route (Matthew 2:12).

The traditional Nativity scene includes a three-sided stable with a star beaming down from above. Inside are Joseph, Mary, and the baby Jesus, a couple of shepherds, a few sheep, a donkey, and the three Wise Men with camels standing in the shadows. The scene captures the main elements of the story in one setting. But the Wise Men actually arrived months later. The stable long forgotten, the Christ child and his family were residing in a house, possibly rented.

A significant thing about the magi is that after meeting the Christ, they returned home "by another route." I too must return to my world, but I will return to it different from when I first came. My way will be changed because I have been changed.

December 27

Show me your ways, o LORD, teach me your paths (Psalm 25:4).

I need fresh direction as I prepare for the year ahead. I must not wait until the night before it arrives. Today I will lift my heart to the Lord, using this prayer of David in today's passage. I want to know God's ways. This comes by revelation though His Word and by His Holy Spirit. He wants me to know His character, the "why" of His behavior. It is an ongoing revelation, always fresh, never boring.

I want to be like Jesus, and this is what He wants for me also. His Spirit is at work in my life, teaching me His paths, which will take me to my highest goal. The process is better than trying to follow a road map. Like the GPS device in my car, the Holy Spirit talks me through my journey. There are no demands but neither are His directions merely suggestions.

My desire is to be like Jesus. "o LORD, teach me your paths."

DECEMBER 28

Go up and down the streets of Jerusalem, look around and consider, search through her squares. If you can find but one person who deals honestly and seeks the truth, I will forgive this city (Jeremiah 5:1).

"If you can find but one person . . ." God's message through Ezekiel was: "I looked for someone who might rebuild the wall of righteousness that guards the land. I searched for someone to stand in the gap in the wall so I wouldn't have to destroy the land, but I found no one" (Ezekiel 22:30 NLT). I am amazed that God said only one person could make such a difference for good. Those must have been terrible times!

A question: If I had lived then, would I have been the one to make the difference? I am quick to notice how bad things are. May I be equally quick to respond to God's request with Isaiah's words, "Here am I. Send me!" (Isaiah 6:8).

DECEMBER 29

From the fullness of his grace we have all received one blessing after another (John 1:16).

"One blessing after another." That phrase accurately expresses my experience with God, as I have not recognized everything as a blessing. Usually I see the good that came out of my experience after the fact, when I take the time to reflect.

A sure way to see my list of blessings grow is to view my life as a cart pulled by God's team of horses, one named Grace and the other, Mercy. They are perfectly matched, strong, untiring, steady, and right on time. I need only ask two questions: What would have happened if I had gotten what I deserved? What good have I received that I didn't deserve? I did not hear the crack of a whip nor did I hear God's whisper direct the details of His blessing to me—one after another!

DECEMBER 30

You came near when I called you, and you said, "Do not fear" (Lamentations 3:57).

I fear both the known and the unknown. I fear going through experiences I've never had before. I fear repeating some experiences. Sometimes it's not the event but what's involved in the process. Comedian Woody Allen said, "I'm not afraid to die, I just don't want to be there when it happens."[3] I laugh along with the rest but there is more truth in the quip than I care to admit.

I remember as a child calling out into the darkness, "Dad?" When his strong voice answered, "What's the matter, pal?" I felt emboldened to say, "I'm scared!" Dad's voice reassured me that a strong, loving father was on the other side of my bedroom wall, awake and ready to come to my aid.

I've cried out to the Lord thousands of times because I was afraid. His answer, "Do not fear."

DECEMBER 31

Teach us to number our days aright, that we may gain a heart of wisdom (Psalm 90:12).

More than one person has lamented, "If I had known I was going to live this long, I would have taken better care of myself." The psalmist wrote that one's life expectancy could stretch seventy to eighty years (Psalm 90:10). That's anywhere from 25,550 to 29,200 days!

I don't know how many more days I have to live. I didn't expect to live as long as I have. Deathclock.com calculates the remainder of one's days based on certain life factors. I checked mine, and it reminds me that my life is slipping away one second at a time.

The psalmist was not being morbid in today's passage. I like the NLT best: "Teach us to make the most of our time, so that we may grow in wisdom."

---

3   Woody Allen. (n.d.). BrainyQuote.com. Retrieved March 9, 2012, from BrainyQuote.com Web site: http://www.brainyquote.com/quotes/quotes/w/woodyallen148186.html

OLD TESTAMENT

Genesis

1:5 / July 14
18:13 / July 26
19:16 / August 24
21:1-2 / August 6
22:14 / October 3
22:16, 18 / July 31
24:1 / November 18
24:15 / March 17
25:22 / July 18
28:15 / April 28
30:20 / September 2
31:7 / January 20
31:20 / July 16
41:52 / May 27
42:1 / August 15

Exodus

1:12 / August 7
3:15 / September 17
4:11 / October 5
4:31 / November 21
6:9 / January 23
14:20 / August 17
15:13 / March 20
16:4 / May 28
18:21-23 / April 29
23:30 / August 10

34:21 / July 6

Leviticus
5:1 / September 18
9:4 / August 9
14:34 / October 7
26:13 / July 3

Numbers
3:38 / July 4
10:29 / August 13
14:20 / September 19
17:8 / October 8
18:6 / November 22
20:12 / August 20
21:4 / March 21
22:32 / May 1
23:10 / January 24
36:6 / September 7

Deuteronomy
3:26 / August 2
4:31 / September 20
5:29 / August 25
8:16 / October 10
8:18 / November 25
11:11-12 / January 1
16:10 / March 24
23:5 / May 3
27:14-26 / August 31
29:29 / June 1
31:19, 21 / September 8
32:51 / August 20
33:12 / January 27

Joshua
1:11 / September 22
3:5 / October 11
5:15 / January 29
9:14 / September 5
13:1 / March 25
22:20 / May 4
23:10 / November 26
24:15 / June 2

Judges
3:2 / August 30
4:14 / September 23
5:21 / November 29
6:13 / February 1
6:14 / May 6
7:2 / June 5
7:4 / March 28
7:21 / October 13

Ruth
(none)

1 Samuel
1:17 / September 9
1:27 / September 25
2:9 / November 30
2:18 / May 8
3:21 / October 14
10:22 / March 29
12:3 / February 2
12:23 / June 6
22:2 / September 4

2 Samuel

1:19, 25, 27 / Sept. 26
1:27 / April 1
6:5 / September 13
6:7 / October 16
6:12-23 / May 11
13:37 / June 7
14:14 / December 3
16:14 / February 5

1 Kings

3:5, 13 / October 17
11:14, 23 / February 7
12:7 / December 4
12:30 / April 2
13:26 / May 12
20:11 / June 8

2 Kings

3:18 / February 10
6:16 / April 4
7:9 / December 6
13:4 / May 16
13:14 / June 11

1 Chronicles

5:22 / September 14
5:24-25 / September 28
10:13 / December 8
16:43 / October 19
25:1 / February 13
28:20 / April 6
29:1 / June 12
29:9 / May 17

2 Chronicles

6:18 / December 22
15:7 / December 10
16:12 / February 16
20:17 / May 20
21:20 / June 14
30:12 / July 11

Ezra

1:5 / December 12
9:4 / February 19
9:13 / April 7

Nehemiah

4:6 / April 10
4:9 / December 15
4:11 / May 13
7:2 / February 20
9:10 / June 17
10:4 / June 15

Esther

(none)

Job

1:22 / April 11
4:3-4 / July 15
9:8 / July 23
9:10 / September 29
11:6 / February 23
13:27 / July 9
14:7-9 / July 29
16:5 / October 20
16:20-21 / August 27

21:2 / June 18
26:14 / December 16

Psalms
1:3 / November 15
5:3 / July 17
8:2 / November 23
9:10 / September 1
13:5 / September 11
17:14 / May 24
18:16 / December 9
18:33 / January 16
18:35 / March 22
18:36 / August 23
20:4 / March 2; Aug. 1
22:25 / September 15
23:2 / January 7
25:4 / Nov. 7; Dec. 27
25:14 / April 3; Oct. 22
27:13 / July 24; Nov. 19
30:1 / November 11
30:11-12 / March 26
31:7 / January 3
31:12 / May 19
31:20 / August 21
31:21 / July 1
34:1-22 / April 8
35:27 / Jan. 10; July 2
40:1 / February 6
50:22 / January 22
50:23 / February 18
52:9 / February 22
54:4 / July 20
55:22 / October 29

57:8 / February 26
62:11-12 / August 29
63:6 / July 28
65:9 / January 13
66:12 / March 10
66:13-14 / December 1
68:19 / February 9
69:4 / January 26
71:14 / August 14
72:15 / April 12
73:17 / December 17
73:28 / November 27
77:14 / December 5
78:4 / May 5
78:72 / January 19
87:7 / Feb. 12; May 10
89:15 / March 30
90:12 / December 31
91:14-16 / August 11
92:15 / October 1
94:17-19 / March 14
100:3 / April 16
104:15 / January 30
105:17 / May 14
105:24 / August 4
105:38 / May 29
107:10 / June 13
107: 20 / February 3
109:4 / September 3
112:7 / August 18
118:15-16 / June 3
118:24 / July 21
119:28 / June 9
119:32 / February 15

119:49-50 /December 20
119:162 / August 26
119:165 / June 26
124:7 / September 6
127:2 / March 6
129:2 / November 4
138:3 / December 13
138:7-8 / April 26
139:5 / July 30
139:16 / August 8
139:18 / April 21
139:20 / March 18
140:7 / April 30
145:16 / June 20

Proverbs
1:23 / October 4
3:18 / October 23
3:24 / December 19
10:7 / February 24
11:25 / July 8
12:25 / April 14
13:20 / June 19
15:4 / February 29

Ecclesiastes
5:3 / October 24
7:16-18 / December 21
8:5-6 / February 27
8:11 / April 15
10:4 / June 22

Song of Solomon
(none)

Isaiah
3:9 / October 26
7:9 / March 1
7:11, 14 / December 23
7:18 / April 18
30:18 / June 23

Jeremiah
3:4-5 / October 27
5:1 / December 28
6:15 / June 24
12:5 / March 4
22:15-16 / April 19
31:16-17 / May 18
39:17 / July 10

Lamentations
1:9 / March 5
3:21-23 / October 28
3:57 / December 30

Ezekiel
13:2 / March 8
13:19 / May 9
16:8 / June 25
16:49 / April 20
31:31 / January 2
35:5 / May 22

Daniel
2:14 / April 23
4:27 / March 9
7:1 / January 5
11:32 / June 27

Hosea
2:15 / October 31

Joel
(none)

Amos
6:5 / November 1

Obadiah
1:15 / November 2

Jonah
1:17; 4:6-8 / November 5
2:8 / January 6

Micah
2:1 / March 12
6:5 / November 6
6:8 / April 24
7:7 / June 28
7:8 / January 9
7:18 / May 23

Nahum
1:7 / November 9

Habakkuk
3:2 / November 10
3:17-18 / January 12

Zephaniah
3:9 / Jan. 14; Nov. 13
3:17 / March 13

Haggai

2:19 / November 14

Zechariah

2:8 / November 17

3:8 / June 29

4:10 / April 25

4:14 / May 26

9:12 / January 17

11:8 / March 16

11:16 / May 31

Malachi

(none)

NEW TESTAMENT

Matthew

2:12 / December 26

9:13 / September 16

10:19 / August 19

21:45 / April 9

28:8 / February 21

Mark

5:36 / September 21

9:30-31 / August 12

Luke

1:38 / December 24

1:45 / July 19

1:58 / September 24

1:74-75 / March 31

2:19, 51 / July 25

5:16 / December 18
5:17 / April 13
6:16 / May 25
7:13 / July 12
14:10 / July 22
18:1 / August 5
22:32 / August 22

John
1:16 / December 29
1:49 / April 17
9:3 / July 7
11:4 / February 17
11:40 / June 30
14:27 / August 16
16:22, 33 / August 3
17:15 / September 27
21:19 / July 5

Acts
3:6 / April 22
7:26 / September 30
11:29 / February 25
13:15 / January 4

Romans
1:12 / October 2
9:17 / January 8
12:12 / February 28
15:30 / April 27

1 Corinthians
1:8 / September 12
1:16 / January 11
1:18 / October 6
2:13 / March 3
4:4 / May 2

2 Corinthians
1:20 / October 9
4:7 / May 7
4:17 / January 15
7:14 / March 7
9:15 / December 25

Galatians
1:24 / July 13
3:4 / September 10

Ephesians
1:16 / July 27
3:16, 18, 20 / October 12

Philippians
1:6 / October 15
1:7 / January 18
1:12 / May 15
1:27 / March 11

Colossians
1:29; 2:1 / October 18

1 Thessalonians
4:11-12 / August 28
4:18 / March 15
5:11 / October 21
5:12-22 / January 21

2 Thessalonians
2:16-17 / October 25
3:17 / January 25

1 Timothy
1:15 / October 30
4:7 / May 21
6:5-6 / January 28

2 Timothy
1:12 / January 31
2:9 / November 3
4:18 / March 19

Titus
2:10 / May 30

Philemon
1:7 / November 8

Hebrews
2:10 / November 12
2:14, 18 / February 4
3:13 / March 23
6:15 / June 4

James

1 Peter

2 Peter

1 John

2 John

3 John

Jude

Revelation